Six Sigma: SPC and TQM in Manufacturing and Services

This book is dedicated to all the customers world-wide who have purchased something, and when they got the item home and opened the box the nightmare began. Perhaps they found that it was broken, parts were missing, it did not work at all, it failed to do what it said on the box or it rapidly broke down. Then perhaps began the hopeless task of dealing with 'customer services': wrong telephone number or always engaged, wrong department and shunted around, not enough or unhelpful staff, inconvenient service appointments, long waits or failed visits, and unsatisfactory or non-existent repair or replacement.

To us, the consumer: it need never be like this.

Six Sigma: SPC and TQM in Manufacturing and Services

GEOFF TENNANT

Gower

Published by
Gower Publishing Limited
Gower House
Croft Road
Aldershot
Hampshire GU11 3HR
England

Gower Publishing Company
131 Main Street
Burlington VT 05401-5600 USA

Reprinted 2001

Geoffrey Tennant has asserted his right under the Copyright, Designs and Patents Act 1988 to be identified as the author of this work.

British Library Cataloguing in Publication Data

Tennant, Geoff
  Six Sigma : SPC and TQM in manufacturing and services
  1. Total quality managment   2. Quality control   3. Quality assurance
  I. Title
  658.5′62

ISBN 0 566 08374 4

Library of Congress Cataloging-in-Publication Data

Tennant, Geoff.
  Six Sigma : SPC and TQM in manufacturing and services / Geoff Tennant.
    p. cm.
  ISBN 0-566-08374-4 (hardback)
   1. Quality control–Statistical methods. 2. Production management–Statistical
  methods. 3. Total quality management. 4. Customer services–Quality control–Statistical
  methods. I. Title.

  TS156 .T45 2000
  658.5′62–dc21
                                       00-042962

Typeset in 9/13pt Utopia by Acorn Bookwork, Salisbury, Wilts.
and printed in Great Britain by T J International Ltd., Padstow.

Contents

List of Figures and Tables

FIGURES

TABLES

Acknowledgements

Although I was involved with the GE Capital Six Sigma quality initiative from early in 1996, it was not until June of that year that I received any formal instruction, when I attended the first ever GE Capital Master Black Belt training in Europe. The first week of four, held in the UK under the direction of Eric Mattenson from Corporate Quality, was truly informative and inspirational. The 24 delegates, from the UK, Europe, Australia and the USA, acknowledged at the time the tremendous input from Corporate Quality and members of the international management consultancy firms who contributed to that first week.

Such was the relative scarcity of information and understanding about Six Sigma quality at that time that developing and delivering extensive in-house training has surely been one of the major reasons for the outstanding success of Six Sigma within General Electric. I have been fortunate not only to receive many such weeks of first-class training, but also to assist with both the development and delivery of Six Sigma quality courses within Europe.

Learning is never more effective than when actively working and training at the cutting edge of a new initiative. The small group formed to launch quality within GE European Equipment Finance under the charismatic leadership of Nicolleta Giadrossi looked back two years later upon some remarkable achievements within our small part of the financial services industry.

Those first two or three years with GE Capital's Six Sigma quality initiative were indeed history in the making. As much as anything else, I acknowledge the fortune to have found myself at exactly the right place at the right time.

G.T.

Introduction

Quality now plays an ever-increasing role in corporate strategy, as global organizations attempt to gain a world-wide market edge by meeting customer needs more effectively, improving internal efficiency and reducing costs. As the marketplace becomes ever smaller, more demanding and more competitive, with customer expectation and product complexity following a never-ending upward path, companies which cannot adapt rapidly while maintaining excellent standards will surely be overtaken by those which can. The positive demonstration of what amounts to perfection, both internally and externally, no longer remains a fanciful dream, but has become essential today, for products and services alike.

What purports to be 'quality' has always been a mix of perhaps fuzzy philosophy and complex statistics, and the gap between rigid control and monitoring in manufacturing and the total lack of any standard for most service industries does little to inspire proactive use of any universal form of quality management. Businesses have for many years realized that customer satisfaction from zero-defect goods and services holds the key to economic success, but the many forms of quality management techniques applied during the last century have failed to provide a simple, proven and easily executable tool or method for common everyday use. Much faith and hope currently rests on varieties of quality assurance, which can provide some standardization of processes and procedures, but generally only control customer-experienced quality by identifying and rejecting out-of-specification products or services. This fails completely to address any of the real causes of the problem, and inevitably passes ownership and responsibility for quality control to employees working within the process, who generally have little wherewithal to ensure a repeatable and successful outcome.

For decades, the principle of 'Murphy's Law' has been universally accepted, and many consumers well know that if something can go wrong, it will, and if something does go wrong, then another failure often quickly follows. However, it required an engineer at Motorola in the 1980s to show formally and conclusively that products failed in the hands of end users more often if defects had needed to be fixed or corrected at some point on the production line at the factory. The converse to this quite unsurprising fact is simple: make or do something right the first time, and the chances are it will not go wrong for the customer later. At that time, Motorola was caught between its high but acceptable level of internal failure and the unarguable external success of competitive Japanese industry in producing similar goods at just a fraction of that failure rate. Thus began a drive for product and corporate quality, firmly targeted at reducing error and defect, which was to give birth to an entirely new approach ultimately known as 'Six Sigma'. Substantially based on already existing well-known tools and techniques from long-established Statistical Process Control and more recently introduced Total Quality Management, the new concept has many critics who challenge both the value and substance of this fresh approach. Many suggest that it is no more than a passing fad from American management consultants, while others decry the fundamental concepts as being totally unsound and without foundation.

Against a backdrop of almost cagey secrecy and contrasting and overtly disapproving conjecture during the 1990s, one of the greatest proponents of Six Sigma has been Jack Welsh, CEO of General

Electric. Perhaps even more enthusiastically than Motorola itself, GE has taken Six Sigma to heart in a frenzied five-year rush to totally transform the organization and strive for world-class quality performance. Lawrence Bossidy, CEO of AlliedSignal, is a strong supporter of the Six Sigma approach, implementing it throughout the organization following the public release by Motorola, in the mid-1990s, of the previously well-guarded secret of how to implement Six Sigma in practice. There had been a long-standing association between Welsh and Bossidy, so early success at Allied-Signal inevitably sparked a similar interest in Welsh, who has spent many years proactively introducing changes to eliminate excessive bureaucracy, inefficiency and poor quality and performance from his own company.

Six Sigma as a quality methodology was quickly adopted and applied across General Electric with a speed and breadth that has at times bordered on mania. There have been many motives behind this undertaking, but this major initiative guaranteed that by 1999 Six Sigma became both better applied and better understood in General Electric than anywhere else. The introduction of Six Sigma to the finance division, GE Capital, brought to a business entirely based on service transactions the alien statistical methods and quality concepts that were more at home in manufacturing. Such a move prompted careful consideration and a full evaluation of such methods, and consequently often led to fresh insights and improved practices. Certainly, no other organization has expended so much effort on customer quality in such a short space of time, and the results are both manifest and substantial.

There is no doubt that a Six Sigma quality approach is achievable in practice and can provide quite outstanding returns on the substantial investment required. The author personally directed a handful of very early Six Sigma projects, which in just one year provided a documented potential for annual savings and revenue increases of more than £250 000. Extend and realize such performance over many projects, year on year, and the benefits suddenly begin to look quite awesome. All of this took place in a financial services company that was already highly efficient, well structured and ISO 9002 accredited. In addition to real bottom-line profit, many intangible and perhaps even radical benefits can be gained from a successful Total Quality Management implementation. Employee involvement and enthusiasm grew from small beginnings, and when even those sceptical of the approach realized that Six Sigma was possible and productive, more and more began to action changes outside the mainstream quality initiative. Processes that had operated poorly or perhaps inappropriately for years, despite general discontent, now became fair game for improvement, and real change was soon observed in every part of the business.

In application, Six Sigma owes much to existing tools and techniques from Total Quality Management and Statistical Process Control, but it introduces a few essential ingredients that catalyse the rest of a weak mixture of customer quality and process improvement to form an almost potentially explosive medium. Six Sigma is a metric that can be applied across any business or organization anywhere for almost any process. It is this one element, above all others, which finally cohesively gels together all the aspects required to action and maintain outstanding product delivery and customer service in fields ranging from the manufacture of plastics to answering a telephone, from shoppers in supermarket queues to invoices and supplier accounts, from light bulbs to aircraft engines, railcars to medical scanners, sales and marketing to accounts and information technology. Because of the very specific goal provided by the Six Sigma metric, every single employee can be empowered to become actively interested and involved, and to participate proactively in providing outstanding quality to the customer. However, the real proof of success must lie with the customers themselves, and there has never been any doubt that both customers and employees noticed real improvements in terms of reductions in defects, enhanced performance of processes, and a decrease in the need to rework errors and remedy omissions and mistakes.

This book addresses a general audience of quality directors, senior management and anyone with an interest in dramatically improving the quality of products or services in both manufacturing and service industries. Some tools from Total Quality Management and Statistical Process Control are introduced and explained, but the principal questions to be addressed are:

- What is Six Sigma all about, and what does it mean?
- Why would my organization be interested in applying Six Sigma?
- Where and how can Six Sigma be used to the best advantage?
- How best can Six Sigma be introduced, and what does it involve?

The rigorous application of Six Sigma requires an eclectic set of knowledge and skills, as well as a sound understanding of customer-centred process management. Even established Six Sigma practitioners may fall into the trap of ignoring the fundamental statistical principles involved, and opt for a simpler definition that is defect-based. There is no doubt that the stretch to meet the targets that Six Sigma performance implies will not be achievable without a corresponding stretch in mind set. This book aims to cut through the controversy, myth and mysticism surrounding Six Sigma, and to explore and explain the fundamental principles and new paradigms of this particular concept of quality, and of its application to business process and product improvement.

Six Sigma is about more than just quality improvement, as it touches the very structure and nature of any organization that may wish to apply such a concept. Due consideration is therefore given to the more intangible and human aspects of the introduction and management of quality. The statistical basis for Six Sigma is fully explained with examples, and a thoroughly practical approach to executing Six Sigma within an organization is followed throughout. Quality philosophy, the nature of added value, customers and customer research, organizational structure and process improvement, and cultural and change management are all explored and discussed. This volume is therefore also highly suitable for use as a general textbook on customer-targeted quality and as a high-level guide to applying Six Sigma in particular, and will appeal to students of business studies, quality management and those seeking a gentle introduction to statistical methods as applied to quality.

What a work such as this cannot easily do is to convey through its pages a sense of the enthusiasm and deep-seated enjoyment that a successful Six Sigma initiative can bring to an organization. There were certainly moments of considerable difficulty and bewilderment, particularly in the very early days when the entire concept was all so fresh and new, and still very much in need of local interpretation and adaptation. It is hoped that this book will spare its readers such anguish, and in so doing allow Six Sigma practitioners the full pleasure that world-class customer satisfaction can bring. It is not just the customer who benefits when everything is done right first time – employee and company pride and satisfaction provide excellent reasons for going to work each day!

CHAPTER ONE

The Development of Quality

Quality is a concept that is very difficult to define. In practice, everyone understands what quality means, and can easily recognize products or services that are either of 'good' quality or of 'bad' quality. The problem comes when trying to gauge quality on an *absolute scale*, rather than just relating one quality standard to another. One dictionary definition of quality is 'grade of goodness', which prompts the question of exactly what 'goodness' is, and how to measure it. The definition of 'goodness', in turn, is 'excellence', and of 'excellence', 'any excellent quality', which leads right back to where we started.

The importance of quality today is as great as it has ever been, if not more so. No company or organization wishes to be associated with poor quality, however it is measured. The gap between one organization and another, between one product and another or between one service and another is generally perceived to relate to the quality of the product or service. Certainly, quality is used by organizations as an essential differentiator, and everyone strives to achieve good or excellent quality at all levels. Even the low-priced end of the marketplace aims for tangible quality – perhaps even more so. The slogan 'quality at low prices' is a well-worn one.

Therefore, what is quality, how does it benefit an organization, how can it be measured, and more importantly, how can it be improved? Perhaps the best way to answer this is to start by looking back in history at how the concept and practice of quality have developed, and the role quality has played within commerce and trade in general.

A basic ground rule that will be applied throughout this book is that 'quality' means 'perceived level of satisfaction as applied to either products or services'. 'Quality' is also a term that can be applied to people and less tangible items such as upbringing or breeding, but that is certainly outside the scope of this book.

QUALITY BEFORE CONSULTANTS

If 'quality' is to be applied only to services and products, then consideration must start with early trade. From prehistoric times, groups of people have exchanged goods to obtain items they themselves cannot make. Early regular trade in the British Isles involved such things as salt, iron nails and millstones. These usually came from the coast and the near Continent, and were exchanged for food and other items of value. Such goods either were not available locally or were of such poor quality as to be of little use. Millstones, used for grinding corn, have to be made from a certain grade and quality of granite, such as is to be found in France, or they wear down too quickly.

Here we have our first hint as to the real meaning of 'quality': *fitness for use*. This can apply to many aspects of a product. To obtain millstones from the Continent required greater initial effort and cost than using local stone, and maintaining a high-quality granite millstone is hard work. The end product for a miller is high-grade flour, but probably more important is the ability to grind without a break in continuity. A miller without a working stone went unused and unpaid, and the local community might starve.

A great deal of early trade took place between Western Europe and the Far East. Incoming goods were numerous, and included spices and fine items like silk. In most cases, these are things that simply cannot be produced locally, so quality is not an issue, it is simply a matter of obtaining the product. Silk and fine cloths were of better quality than homespun cloth, but if 'fitness for use' is the best definition of 'quality', it is inadequate in this instance. At that time, cloth was used to cover, protect, keep warm, and it needed to be hard-wearing. Silk from the Orient will neither wear as well nor perform most practical tasks better than locally produced cloth, but more often than not it is described as a quality product.

Most modern concepts of quality are allied to 'fitness for use', a term used by Joseph Juran and quality consultants since, so where have we gone wrong? The difficulty here is that quality is often falsely associated with *luxury*, and we may have missed the real purpose for which a product is used. Fine silk is a luxury product, used to convey wealth as much as for practical purposes, and the better 'fitness for use' of silk must surely be that it is nicer to wear and look at, even if it is less practical.

As craftsmanship and trade developed during the Middle Ages, elaborate structures grew to control and protect both producers and consumers alike. Craft guilds were established to oversee young people beginning to learn a trade as apprentices, and jobbers or improvers developing their skills by moving from job to job. Once a craftsman felt that he had learnt his trade, he applied to the guild to be recognized as a master of his craft. This required the presentation of a *masterpiece*: the best-quality item the craftsman could make using all his skill and talent. This was never intended for sale or use, so as an item it was free from any perceptions of 'fitness for use' or 'luxury', but instead had to convey a deep sense of quality in the purest sense of the term. Quality here must surely be in the eye of the beholder: seen by only the master craftsmen of the guild, it was the final proof of the quality of a man's craftsmanship, which in turn implied the quality of what he would produce. Only once the guild were satisfied with the quality of workmanship would a man be elevated to master craftsman status and allowed to take on apprentices himself.

If we further consider services in the past, we again encounter difficulties in defining 'quality'. Probably the earliest service rendered by one individual to another was slavery, and services of a more personal kind. Not wishing to dwell on such subjects, other examples that are more recent would include early forms of transport. Moving someone or something from A to B has no product, so it is entirely a service rendered. In many cities in the eighteenth century, sedan chairs or bath chairs were a popular form of transport (as they still are in many parts of the world), and quality and luxury are both terms that can be applied to this service. To travel first class rather than second or standard class implies luxury rather than quality, and at first glance it may be difficult to see how quality can be applied to this situation at all. The British invented the tip, initially associated with the transport of goods, and now applied to almost any service. A tip (which some have taken to stand for 'To Insure Promptness') was originally a sum of money paid in advance to improve or guarantee the quality of a service. To travel by sedan chair is luxury compared with walking or riding a horse, but once a passenger had chosen to travel this way, to arrive quicker than usual was seen as a quality service. Again quality – here equated with speed – is measured in the eye of the beholder. The differentiation is that to travel with an experience of comfort is a measure of *luxury*; to arrive satisfied with the outcome is a measure of *quality*.

To attempt to separate the concept of luxury from quality, it is proposed that people *choose in advance the level of luxury* they require from a service or product, and that they *experience quality as a level of satisfaction* with the service or product. The phrase 'you only get what you pay for' is generally taken to imply that quality (satisfaction with the outcome) is related to cost (the input).

This is simply not so, as it is luxury that is related to cost; we buy luxury, and the more we pay, the more we get in terms of materials, goods, durability, time and service, and so on. Quality and luxury may apply to the same thing, in that a customer may pay for a more luxurious service or product and therefore expect better quality. However, quality is totally independent, as a concept, to both cost and luxury. Quality is related to the satisfaction experienced from a product or service, and certainly satisfaction has roots deep in such considerations as fitness for use, but also more ethereal and intangible concepts. 'Satisfaction' has many dictionary definitions, but one is 'to give content', which matches quite well with 'goodness', and it is the author's belief that quality is best defined as *satisfaction experienced*. Is it possible to buy quality, and thus relate cost and quality? At first sight it may seem so, but in looking deeper we will see that this is not the case.

In times past, producing goods for sale and providing services were, before the Industrial Revolution, very much a local affair. With very close customer contact, organizations were brought into being with a strong customer service ethic, and it was the customer who ultimately controlled quality. In the past, to increase the revenue obtained from a product or service meant increasing the level of luxury offered. To stay in business meant maintaining the high level of quality customers expected. Following the Industrial Revolution, when workers moved to factories and items began to be mass-produced and marketed at a distance, organizations grew in size and came into being for more financial reasons. With this, financial controls became more important, and it was possible to increase revenue by adjusting quality as well as luxury. In the distant past, more money was made by leaving more cream in the milk and charging more. During the nineteenth and twentieth centuries, more money was made by adding water to the milk or by investing in a machine to cut out the milkmaid.

AMERICAN QUALITY DISCOVERED

During the Victorian period, manufacturers did everything possible to improve profits without regard for quality. Strange and dangerous substances were added to food products that would, literally, make hair curl, all in pursuit of delivering a 'better' product at a certain price. Competing railway companies cut services and facilities to the point where it was unpleasant to travel. Numerous manufacturing industries turned out products in any way possible and with disregard for employee safety, as long as there was a satisfactory return on investment. During this period, some of the greatest legislative changes ever seen in the UK were introduced to force organizations to meet acceptable standards in health, education, welfare, commerce and trade.

Running right through to the present day, it has become the duty of public officers, rather than organizations themselves, to devise, legislate and monitor standards of quality in all fields of life. In direct contrast to the earlier rush for free trade, state ownership of such areas as railways slowly began to redress standards to ensure a level of quality in products and services. This has been most notable in areas of public safety and health. Organizations that are run for fiscal reasons only, and with little regard for customers and employees, naturally tend to compromise on all aspects of quality unless and until such actions begin to visibly hurt the bottom-line profit.

Eventually a balance is arrived at, where organizations provide products and services to a level of quality that meets publicly accepted and enforced standards, and yet still return a handsome profit. Over time, public satisfaction with such standards may change, thus driving a move towards new legislation and a slight shift in the balance, until the *status quo* returns. Concerns over safety aspects of recently privatized railways in the UK have shown that this is still much the case.

Against this background of 'accept unless pushed', the beginning of the twentieth century found one or two individuals conducting statistical research in the UK into improved methods of agriculture. In particular, Ronald Fisher was working at Rothamsted Experimental Station during the 1920s. The use of statistics as a mathematical tool had developed relatively late in the nineteenth century, and was now further developed to help optimize crop rotation and planting techniques. With so many variations in soil, fertilizer, planting, watering and weather and so on, it required statistical hypothesis-testing to identify whether crop A had really produced better than crop B. This practical use of statistics to identify 'best practice' inspired Walter Shewhart at Bell Laboratories in the USA. Shewhart developed the use of statistical methods to monitor and thus control processes during the 1930s. His work has evolved over the years into what is now the widely accepted use of 'control charts', and was adopted by manufacturing industries in America long before 1950. This was pioneering work, attempting to identify what defined a successful process, and then monitoring and controlling the process to ensure continued acceptable quality.

From this early beginning, W. Edwards Deming and Joseph Juran, now both father figures of the American quality movement, developed a deep understanding of quality and the pursuit of perfection by applying quality principles and techniques to processes, and also to the management of organizations. Indeed, the work of Deming is as much to do with management practice as it is to do with producing and making things. A great believer in the value of the individual, Deming devised 14 points for management, more than half of which are concerned with employees. He is often quoted as remarking that 'eighty-five percent of the reasons for failure ... are related to deficiencies in systems and processes ... rather than the employee'. Against this, however, America was gearing up for a mass consumer market as never before. The golden age of manufacturing in the USA was dawning, and there was money to be made, just from making things. Deming and others working towards a better understanding of quality practices and methods found their ideas not overtly welcomed. They were working in an America that was dominating world manufacturing, and had almost no rivals. With almost no practical interest in their work at home, they were invited to lecture on quality in Japan.

QUALITY GOES JAPANESE

Japanese culture is poles apart to that of America. For the Japanese, concepts of the work ethic, business 'fair play', respect for authority and social structure are almost diametrically opposed to what we are accustomed to in the West. Japan had sprung onto the world arena, from an isolated but advanced culture, during the latter part of the nineteenth century. With a technology base that was culturally frozen in time and a burning desire to adopt anything alien from the West, it was not long before centuries of Western development were being consumed, analysed and adopted. When first exposed to the West, Japan had no modern ship-designing skills, unlike the UK, which had many large shipyards. Without the British sense of 'cricket and fair play', Japanese companies asked for plans of ships they 'intended to buy'. Once obtained, plans were copied and returned, and negotiations ceased. The Japanese then built the ships themselves, much to the shock and horror of the British. Fair play was restored when the Japanese tried this again – plans were subtly adjusted so that the ships sank when built. The Japanese then started to design ships themselves, and ultimately to do it better, cheaper and to a higher level of quality than anyone else.

In a culture where the guest or customer is treated with utmost respect, where employees have a life-long association with the company, and where it is second nature to observe, copy and improve, the concept of quality introduced by Deming spread rapidly. It is interesting to note that the uptake of such ideas was probably very much to do with the employees themselves. In America, as in the UK, trade union resistance to measuring production and resulting quality (time and motion studies) prevented supervisory staff using already known quality practices. In Japan, everyone generally did what the boss wanted almost without question, so quality circles became the second item on the agenda, just after the company work-out and song first thing in the morning.

The result is now legendary. From a standing start, by the 1970s manufacturing industry in Japan was producing cars, motorcycles and domestic goods cheaper than anyone else. Added to that, such items were becoming much nicer to use, and of a better quality. Cars were more reliable, easier to service, ran better, and incorporated more user facilities. During that period, Japan came to dominate the world market by delivering better-quality goods, and then to begin to develop new areas of excellence. Rank Xerox developed photographic reproduction in the early 1960s, and held the world market during the life of the xerography patent. Traditionally, optical lenses made in Japan had been of poor quality, but once the patent expired, Japan began to produce photocopiers which were smaller, cheaper and gave improved performance. As the technology involved began to advance, it was not the innovative West that held the lead, but the methodical and rigorous Eastern countries that steadily advanced the performance of electrical goods through applied quality control. This is where quality really matters. The secret that the Japanese had stumbled onto was that by controlling quality, manufacturing could also reduce defects and wasted costs. Make a component work first time, and there is no expensive repair and fix. The corollary to this is also simple but revolutionary: customers prefer goods that do not break, and really like goods that do what they want them to do.

The West was busy still adding *luxury* to everything, to be able to charge more and increase profits. The East was busy adding *quality* to everything, to be able to produce items better and cheaper. Luxury, as a purchase in itself, tends to be socially driven. By 1980, the stigma of Far East imports had begun to wane and there was almost no reason to buy anything but the cheap, good-quality and very appealing goods flooding the world markets.

QUALITY RETURNS TO AMERICA

Cars and refrigerators are one thing, electrical consumer goods are another. Large, luxurious and locally manufactured cars can compete with smaller imported versions. Even if someone else can make it cheaper, by the time it is imported the added value of the luxury element can sway the customer. However, when manufacturing microelectronics for commerce, it is quality and not luxury that has the final say. Make a million microprocessors, and every one that fails costs money. This is a manufacturing process where the final product either works or it does not, where the costs associated with manufacture are fully expended on every chip, whether it works or not, and where failure after manufacture is hugely expensive. If you make a car and the windscreen wipers fail, the customer will generally have it fixed at their own expense. The cost of the fix is small compared to the revenue generated by the sale of the car. The customer may be annoyed, but the car still works. Make a computer, and if the microprocessor fails, the computer is useless. The cost of the fix is vast compared to the revenue from the initial sale, and may even outweigh the original profit margin.

In Silicon Valley, microelectronic chips were being made with what was felt to be an acceptable failure rate, but in Japan, firms started to produce components with a failure rate 10, 100, even 1000 times smaller. Large computer manufacturers had a choice: buy a million chips from America, and watch 50 000 computers fail during the first year, or buy a million chips from Japan, and watch 500 computers fail. Not a difficult choice to make, and soon American manufacturers were in some difficulty. Traditional quality methods implied that to reduce the defects shipped, every chip had to be tested after it was made. Testing each chip adds considerably to the cost, and for complex computer chips, out of every 10 made, only 2 or 3 may actually work. The Japanese manufacturers, on the other hand, were producing final chips that were more reliable, and the successful production yield was better. Testing is not required if the product is known to work. It is far better to produce a million microprocessors with a known failure rate of 0.1 per cent in the first place than to produce over a million with a failure rate of 6 per cent and have to pick out the good 94 per cent.

Against this competitive backdrop, companies such as Motorola turned again to quality methods, and went back to the Japanese to learn the secrets of their excellent-quality production. During a period of over ten years from the mid-1980s, a consortium including Motorola developed its own quality approach, based on the best elements taken from existing quality ideas dating back to the 1950s, and from current Japanese practices. Ultimately called *Six Sigma*, this concept of a quality *metric* was peculiar to Motorola for many years, although the American motor car manufacturing industry had for some time used four-and-a-half sigma as the standard. Since the sigma quality concept has become more widely known and adopted, several organizations have devised sigma methodologies as a way of introducing and attaining Six Sigma or a similar level of quality.

Over the past forty years, a variety of quality methods have passed through manufacturing industry. Not to be left behind, service industries have adopted Japanese and American flavours of Total Quality Management and ISO standards in a bid to improve quality and profits. Although it is relatively early days, Six Sigma quality has been adopted by a relatively small number of important American companies aspiring to world-class status. In particular, General Electric adopted Six Sigma as their quality improvement methodology in 1995. The General Electric finance services division, GE Capital, was not long in following. By early 1996, it was the first totally service transaction-based company in the world to apply this methodology. Success has followed rapidly, and impressive financial returns have been demonstrated throughout General Electric. By addressing all aspects of quality improvement, implementation and management, the use of Six Sigma quality has demonstrated what will no doubt turn out to be a long-term success story and the beginning of a new chapter in the application of quality.

SUMMARY

- Quality is difficult to define, but is perhaps best considered as *customer satisfaction experienced.*
- Luxury and quality are two different aspects of products and services. Consumers choose a level of luxury against the degree of cost, and independently experience quality as a level of *satisfaction.*
- The history of the development of quality practice is a century old, and no single country, organization or group has retained a monopoly on best practice.
- Six Sigma quality is a recent development in the light of intense competition. Culminating in a desire to produce products (and services) with zero defects, it has been developed by bringing together the best in existing quality methodologies and improvement practices.

CHAPTER TWO

What is Six Sigma?

Six Sigma is many things, and it would perhaps be easier to list all the things that Six Sigma quality is *not*. Six Sigma can be seen as:

- a vision;
- a philosophy;
- a symbol;
- a metric;
- a goal;
- a methodology.

In contrast, Six Sigma is not:

- a cure for all ills;
- a guarantee of success;
- just for manufacturing;
- a simple tool.

Six Sigma is founded upon complex issues, and has evolved to become very much an all-encompassing management tool for change and customer quality. One of Six Sigma's strengths compared to other quality approaches is that it is not just a method, but also the vision, the goal and the symbol all rolled into one. Total Quality Management (TQM) is a much-favoured quality methodology which contributes greatly to the Six Sigma approach. However, TQM does not have a clear aim towards which participants slowly but surely move, and it certainly does not have a firm measure or yardstick by which progress can be monitored. If quality is the aim of any organization, then this aim must be converted into something much more tangible to which each member of that organization can aspire. Further, it must be possible to know when the vision has been attained, and to have a clear path to follow.

Six Sigma brings nothing overtly new to the quality table, except perhaps for two things. Firstly, the name and symbol of Six Sigma itself, almost like a brand name, have the power to draw interest and provide a clear badge that can be affixed to any quality initiative. Much like ISO 9000, 6σ may become the much-prized mark of world-class quality. It is also a metric, and emphasizes the ability to measure a level of quality attainment as a number. Secondly, Six Sigma brings a new paradigm to quality. It has gathered together many of the spoken, inherent views of many groups and individuals, and now firmly proclaims a model to explain the real meaning of quality – *total customer satisfaction.*

The name and banner of Six Sigma subsume a collection of methodologies or practices, tools and techniques aimed at successfully implementing such changes as are required to deliver this new concept of Six Sigma quality. The success of such Six Sigma quality initiatives clearly shows that, as an initiative *and* a methodology, there exists within all of this the necessary substance to successfully execute the new paradigm. The component parts of a Six Sigma quality initiative include:

- Total Quality Management, which provides tools and techniques to bring about cultural change and process improvement within an organization;
- Statistical Process Control (SPC), which supplies powerful metrics, analysis tools and control mechanisms;
- a Japanese approach to process improvement and design, customer satisfaction and customer-needs analysis, helping to bridge the gap between quality as 'satisfaction experienced' and an actionable reality;
- a new paradigm of total customer satisfaction as a primary driver for the quality initiative.

To answer the question 'What is Six Sigma?' therefore requires three answers. It is a new paradigm of customer satisfaction, it is a statistically based measurement scale, and it is a methodology by which quality can be improved. It is definitely not simply a shift in statistical methods and accounting from 'three sigma' to 'six sigma'.

THE NEW PARADIGM

The slogan modified and adopted by GE Capital for its Six Sigma quality initiative is: 'completely satisfying customer needs profitably'. Again, it can be seen that quality has been defined in terms of satisfaction, and also in terms of the customer. Customer satisfaction in itself is not a new concept, as many small businesses are alive, well and thriving because they provide exactly what their customers require. However, the medium- to large-sized organizations of today have become distanced from the customer ethic, and globalization and mass marketing will only continue this trend and drive a wedge between customer and organization. What are companies created for? Profit, simply and bluntly. Without profit, a company can no longer operate, as the creation of the organization generally requires raising money from shareholders, and it is shareholder value that must continue to grow year on year. Any organization that fails to make satisfactory returns from investment faces take-over or decline.

Look at any profit-oriented organization today and you will find that fiscal controls are at the heart of the business. In manufacturing, there will certainly be someone on the production line checking that the widgets are all the correct size, but back in the office will be a team of people monitoring accounts day after day. At the end of every fiscal year, it is the balance sheet that is reported and analysed. If any measure of customer satisfaction strays into the picture, it will be from shareholders expressing pleasure at a sizeable dividend. Ask any company why it is taking over another company, and the reply will always be: 'To return a better financial dividend on the investment of the shareholders.' Non-profitmaking organizations are also subject to tight fiscal control, as there is rarely the opportunity to increase income, only to control expenditure.

So where does the customer fit into this picture? More often than not, the customer has become a means to an end, and not the end itself. The organization sells goods and/or services to a group of almost hapless customers, and in the process makes money. This is the very acceptable face of capitalism, but what drives this process – the customer or the profit? Some large retail stores in the UK have a person at the door greeting customers, and everyone generally feels uncomfortable as a result. In Japan, however, the customer is highly valued, and in many large department stores dedicated staff stand at the foot of escalators, hour after hour, greeting honourable customers as they pass by. An accepted part of the Japanese culture, this view of the customer as central to business runs throughout every organization, and has been a major element in the success of quality, and of Japanese industry in general. Six Sigma is very firmly founded in this tradition, and there is little to be gained in considering Six Sigma further unless an organization is prepared and able to shift the focus of the business to the customer.

For instance, consider the National Health Service in the UK. This is not a profit-related organization, indeed quite the opposite, as fiscal control is principally targeted at controlling costs. Neither is it particularly customer-focused, but perhaps rather result-focused. The principal aim of the NHS is to cure people of ills, not to make money. Take the same market and add profit, and this becomes the private healthcare industry. Suddenly, the business becomes customer-focused; private healthcare is sold as convenience, speed, comfort and privacy, often with little mention of the physical issues involved.

An example of currently successful and profitable customer-focused management is the supermarket chain Tesco. In the 1980s, this organization might have been profit- and result-driven, aiming to sell grocery goods at a low cost with an acceptable profit margin. During the later 1990s, a visible change took place in the way Tesco dealt with customers, and many of the recent service improvements are entirely customer-driven. To be able to return grocery items for a full refund, without question, was almost unheard of in the 1980s. Getting money back from any organization has always been an uphill struggle, but something that many customers both need and want to be able to do. The ability to buy with confidence means that if customers do not like a product or it is not quite right, they can take it back, whatever the reason. Some organizations at the upper end of the retail consumer market have offered this facility for a long time, and been able to justify the costs involved, for example Marks and Spencer. The breakthrough occurred when the lower end of the market realized that by focusing on the customer and meeting customer needs, profit was actually increased, not lost. If the goods sold are acceptable, not many will be returned, but for those customers who do return items, loyalty and brand buy-in can be enormous. Customers will often buy more items as a result, knowing that the purchase can easily be reversed if desired.

In the final analysis, it is the customer who buys the goods and services. Completely satisfy all your customers' needs, and they will beat a path to your door, and not your competitors'. It is wise to add the word *profitably* here, as there is little point in pandering to whims and fancies for small returns; organizations still have to make a profit, as does any successful quality initiative. From the Six Sigma methodology, it is therefore necessary to derive sound financial return, at the same time as exceptional customer satisfaction.

THE METHODOLOGY OF SIX SIGMA

The one facet of Six Sigma that most confuses statisticians and quality assurance employees from the area of manufacturing is the implied use of the term 'Six Sigma' for a process improvement *methodology*. For those who understand 'three sigma' as both a quality target and statistical metric, the extension to six sigma seems to hold no more value and complexity than a movement of the line drawn in the sand marking the acceptable from the unacceptable. In the English language, the word 'hoover' has moved from being a particular brand of vacuum cleaner to being a verb meaning the application of any such machine to the task of cleaning – 'a hoover, I hoover'. Similarly, the phrase 'Six Sigma' has rapidly moved from being just a metric and the title for a fresh alternative approach to being the envelope for all that Six Sigma and an associated quality initiative stands for, including a methodology for implementation. Concepts can often be ethereal and difficult to relate to, particularly when many complex issues or totally new aspects are involved. It is quite natural to shift our understanding towards a more practical realization of the intangible concept, and over time the practical becomes associated with the conceptual, right down to the use of the same name.

Over time, it is expected that 'Six Sigma' will gain the status afforded to a dictionary entry in the 'Oxford English' language. Because it is colloquially acceptable to muddy the difference between nouns, verbs and adjectives, this will require several entries to cover the metric, the philosophy, the concept and the practical application as a methodology through which the ideals of 'Six Sigma' can be attained. Likewise, how the concept of Six Sigma is realized in actuality should not necessarily be restricted to one practical method alone. The vision of Six Sigma is 'excellent quality in the total satisfaction of customer needs', and this could be delivered in reality by very many and assorted means derived from various philosophies. The foundation of the ideals behind Six Sigma does lie heavily within Statistical Process Control and manufacturing, but this in itself does not imply that such tools are either obligatory or necessarily sole prerequisites for success.

To achieve total customer satisfaction, and thus excellent quality, requires practical changes in three key areas: the *customer*, the *process* and the *employee*. To achieve customer satisfaction demands a deep understanding of the customer and a clear benchmark of customer needs and requirements, as has been discussed above. To then be able to deliver to this benchmark calls for business processes (often changed and improved) that have the capability to produce within customer-defined limits. To change, and to do so rapidly and effectively, requires that all employees are working for continuous improvement as well as daily compliance. Whatever mix of tools and techniques is eventually adopted by any one organization in any one Six Sigma methodology, it must include an element of customer analysis, process improvement, metrics and statistics, and cultural change and adaptation to the aspired goal. It is not surprising, therefore, that Six Sigma has grown from manufacturing industries where process metrics and continual improvement are commonplace. The radical shift has been to incorporate into pure process statistics the elements of excellent customer service and employee and management cultural change, and any methodology that aspires to achieving Six Sigma must retain a sound balance in all these areas. Six Sigma methodologies are about organizational change (cultural and procedural), processes (design and improvement), customers (focus on and analysis of), metrics (statistics, performance and targets) and, of course, employees (training, motivation and involvement).

It is true that Six Sigma uses the term 'sigma' in a way that is more akin to a new philosophy of management, rather than a metric to express deviation about the mean or average. The heartfelt pleas of manufacturing quality statisticians to 'separate procedure and process, management and project' are understandable, but must be very firmly rejected. Successful management strategies, change and quality methodologies – Six Sigma included – must contain elements from many areas of expertise, and it is no longer acceptable to say: 'I measure, you manage.'

THE STATISTICAL BASIS OF SIX SIGMA

The revolution that Six Sigma attempts to bring to quality involves a scientific and repeatable fact-based process that enables organizations to measure quality and process improvement on a common scale.

Neither statistics nor science are particularly appealing subjects for most people, and at this point the impatient reader may feel the urge to skip forward to more entertaining chapters. However, applying Six Sigma correctly requires an understanding of the basic principles by all staff in an organization.

Processes

Everything we do is a process, from making a cup of tea to providing a service to a customer. Figure 2.1 shows the basic elements of any such process.

This is often called a SIPOC map: Suppliers of Inputs to a Process that adds value and delivers Outputs to Customers. Processes have characteristics that can, in the main, easily be measured, such as time taken and volume or value of whatever passes through the process: for example, the process of paying for grocery items at a checkout in a supermarket, where the process starts when a customer joins the queue, and stops as the customer heads for the exit. The input to the process is a shopping trolley or basket of goods, and the supplier of this input is the customer. Often in service processes, the supplier of the input to the process is the same as the customer of the output. There may also be more than one input, such as method of payment in this instance, again supplied by the customer. The process goes through a number of sequential, high-level steps, in this case generally being:

1 queue;
2 unload trolley/basket;
3 pre-negotiations (greeting, questions, and so on);
4 scanning;
5 re-load trolley/basket;
6 post-negotiation and payment.

The inputs here have measures, such as the number of items in a basket, the arrival rate of customers in the queue, and the method of payment proffered. The process itself has many internal measures, such as time taken to scan items, number of scanning errors, value of total purchase, and so on. The output of the process is a completed purchase transaction and receipt, and a trolley, basket or bag that can be taken away from the store. Attached to both the inputs and the outputs are requirements and characteristics. The process itself requires certain things from the input: for example, to be successfully scanned, the items presented must be correctly bar-coded, and must also have prices associated with them on the store's computer system. The customer's requirements about the output may include such things as accuracy in the receipt, and all the soft, squashy items being packed at the top of the shopping bag.

Six Sigma quality requires that the customer is totally satisfied with this process, and later we

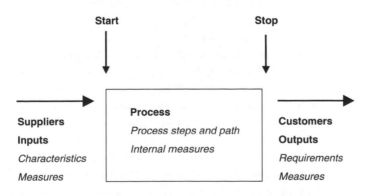

Figure 2.1 The SIPOC map

will explore how best to find out exactly what would satisfy the customer, and how to turn this into a related measurement. For the moment, assume that speed is an essential factor in customer satisfaction, and that the interest is in measuring the time taken to complete this process. It is usually quite possible to measure the time taken between the start and end of the purchasing part of the process – steps 3, 4 and 5 above. With modern computerized cash registers, timing from commencement of scanning to the closure of the cash drawer at end of payment is very easy to measure and analyse accurately. Calculating the queuing time requires observation, which has cost and effort implications, but perhaps provides a more accurate assessment of the customer's experience of this process.

The outcome of interest – here, the time taken for the process to be completed – could be measured for hundreds of customers, and the results collated and analysed. It would be found that there exists a considerable variation in the outcome, and it is this variation that is the fundamental issue within Six Sigma quality. Traditionally, measurements such as these have been taken and then averaged. Indeed, a recently issued membership renewal notice for a UK motoring breakdown organization stated that 'customers are fixed on average within 22½ minutes', which sounds impressive, but misses out entirely the statistic of how much *variation* there is in this figure. Every process is affected by variation, which falls into one of two classes. *Natural variation* occurs because of a number of inherent factors, acting totally at random and independent of each other. This type of variation can be measured and controlled, and perhaps even reduced, but never eliminated. *Non-natural*, or *special cause variation*, occurs because of a (often small) number of non-random factors influencing the processes. As long as the causes for non-natural variation can be identified, this type can usually be fully eliminated. Whichever sort of variation we are dealing with, the statistics are quite simple, in that the outcome almost always follows a well-known pattern, that of the *normal distribution*.

The normal distribution

It is one of the amazing facts of this universe that practically anything anyone would care to measure about any repeated processes or outcome exhibits much the same characteristics. When a frequency distribution of an outcome is formed, by plotting the number of outcomes against the value of interest, the result is almost always a curve with the basic shape shown in Figure 2.2.

In textbooks, the shape is usually drawn as a perfect 'bell curve', whereas in reality it is often misshapen to some degree or other. In Figure 2.2, the histogram was plotted from randomly generated data, and then a smoothed line was plotted over this, highlighting the underlying shape of the distribution.

Why is this curve so important? The answer is that it has two basic characteristics. The first is the average, or arithmetic mean, usually called the *mean* and expressed as μ (mu, the Greek letter m). This is the centre line of the distribution; half of the outcomes fall below it, and half above it. In the example in Figure 2.2, the mean is close to 22, half the area under the curve is below 22, and half above. The second is the measure of variation in the distribution. It can be seen that most of the curve extends out between about 6 and 38 on either side of the mean. In fact, the curve shape is such that it continues to get closer to zero, but never quite reaches it. Other than the mean, there is only one point on the curve that can be identified easily: the point where it turns from convex to concave. Here, where the slope of the curve switches, is a point that defines for each normal distribution the spread of the curve. Known as the *standard deviation*, and often expressed as σ (sigma, the Greek letter s), the distance between the mean and this point is the

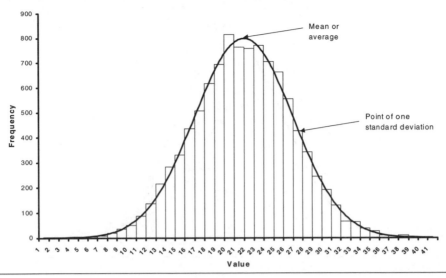

Figure 2.2   Random data showing a normal distribution pattern

value used to define how much variation (variance or deviation from the mean) exists in the distribution. In Figure 2.2, this point is at about 27 (and also at 17), meaning that the value of one standard deviation, one sigma, is approximately five units (27 – 22).

The normal distribution is well understood, at least by mathematicians, and no matter what the curve actually looks like, every curve obeys the following rules:

● The average or mean has half the outcomes above and half below.
● Within a distance of one standard deviation (one sigma) on either side of the mean, 68 per cent of all outcomes are found.
● Within a distance of three sigma-values on either side of the mean, 99.7 per cent of all outcomes are to be found.

Looking at the example in Figure 2.2, almost the entire curve sits within three sigma, or 15 points either side of 22. Now, armed with both the mean and the value for sigma, we are better able to see whether this process satisfies our customer. If, for example, the customer wanted the value to always be below 30, then the average value of 22 would satisfy this requirement. Note, however, that part of the curve falls above the value of 30, and a proportion of our customers will be dissatisfied. In this case, it is possible to show that this process operates at about three sigma, with almost a 7 per cent failure rate.

This is the statistical basis for Six Sigma as a quality metric:

1 For each key customer process, identify the critical measurement or measurements that relate to quality, and the associated acceptable customer limit or limits.
2 Measure each process metric, plot a distribution, and then identify how much of this distribution falls outside the customer's limits. This figure can be quantified as the number of sigma-values between the mean and the given limit (see Figure 2.3).

It can be shown that a process performing at a metric of three sigma encloses approximately 93 per cent of all outcomes, meaning that just 7 in every 100 customers are dissatisfied. If, in the past, quality had been measured in this way, it could have been called 'Three Sigma'. At three sigma,

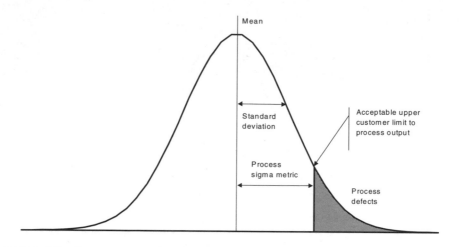

Figure 2.3   Defects as a tail of a normal distribution

there is approximately a 7 per cent failure rate – *only* 7 per cent, but when making one million microchips, that amounts to 66 800 failures. To stretch the target, Motorola aimed very high indeed. To move the goal forward to the very best possible, Six Sigma aims at zero defects. However, because the normal distribution curve goes on and on, never quite reaching zero, a practical limit must be found. At a metric of six rather than three sigma-values either side of the mean – double what has been acceptable practice up to now – almost all outcomes are enclosed, leaving a margin for error of just 3.4 defects per million opportunities.

To achieve Six Sigma, the practical task is to change each core process so that:

- the distribution of each critical measure is centred between the upper and lower customer limits;
- variation in the critical measure is reduced, so that the distance between the centre and either customer limit is at least six standard deviations.

Application to Six Sigma

The practical steps required to fully implement Six Sigma now come into focus. Firstly, in order to be able to identify the current process sigma metric, the following tasks need to be completed:

1 Identify every business function or process.
2 Know and understand the customers of the business.
3 Distinguish the core processes that add value for the customers.
4 For each such core process, obtain specific customer requirements by survey and analysis.
5 Convert process customer requirements into a small number of well-specified, actionable and measurable Critical To Quality (CTQ) characteristics for the process.
6 Measure every CTQ process metric, and for each determine the equivalent normal distribution plot.
7 Overlay onto the plot the customer CTQ limits, and calculate the number of defects outside these limits.
8 Convert this to a process sigma metric.

As can be seen, a considerable amount of work is necessary just to arrive at this point, but the procedure only needs to be completed once, and the organization would then probably understand more about itself than it ever had before. Success in implementing Six Sigma hinges on being able to achieve the above and introduce cultural change at the same time, since point 5 on this list is highly subjective and difficult to carry out unless a decisive, customer-centric approach is adopted.

Six Sigma, as both a metric and a quality methodology, has its weaknesses, and one of them is the total reliance on the subjective and *ad hoc* methods used to arrive at good CTQs. The problem is this: if the customers of the service department require the telephone to be answered quickly, and customer survey leads to a CTQ of 'answer all calls in three rings', then that is what must be delivered in order to achieve excellent quality. If everyone internally knows that currently this is impossible, then there will be internal pressure to set the CTQ at five, seven or even more rings, closer to what can be achieved today. This has a dramatic effect on the calculated process sigma metric, as well as lowering the target. Publicly admitting failure, even internally in a company, is neither socially nor politically comfortable. Setting CTQ limits correctly requires *absolutely and without compromise* a customer-centric vision that hands the task of defining what is acceptable over to the customer. It is unpleasant to discover, after perhaps twenty years of running an organization, that half of what we do is not important to the customer, and that the other half that matters does not amount to much!

At this point in the journey towards Six Sigma, an organization would have a benchmark for each process sigma metric. Process improvements can now begin in earnest, and the best place to start is by identifying which processes need attention – not necessarily those with the lowest sigma metric, but perhaps those with the best financial or customer impact and return, or even the easiest to improve in practice. In order to improve any one process CTQ, the following steps are normally undertaken:

1 Identify, at a business level, the particular process and CTQ to be improved.
2 Perform initial investigation work (and re-evaluate the choice of project).
3 Charter an improvement project team, and document the existing situation.
4 Gather measurements from the process.
5 Analyse the measurements, and look for the root causes of defects.
6 Generate solutions, implement improvements, and measure the change.
7 Return the improved process to the business and controlling ownership.

These actions are undertaken by a quality process improvement team, and it is quite normal for one such team to improve the sigma metric of a process by one point or more. For example, starting with a process benchmarked as operating at two-and-a-half sigma as a metric, one cycle of process improvement could increase this to three-and-a-half sigma, or even better. By repeating the above cycle more than once, the sigma metric of a process can be inched forward towards the aspired goal of Six Sigma. For quality improvement teams to be successful, an organization must also invest training, time and resources in the initiative.

There are very few visible processes world-wide currently operating at a process metric of Six Sigma or better, but here is one acceptable definition of a world-class Six Sigma organization:

> All core processes (which add value for the customer) operate at a metric of four-and-a-half sigma or better, and the organization is actively pursuing quality improvement with the goal of becoming Six Sigma in all of these processes.

The value of implementing Six Sigma as a quality methodology should now be apparent:

- An organization will move to a customer-centric vision, and be actively engaged in continuous and customer-based quality improvement.
- All critical core tasks are seen as customer processes and not business functions, and are monitored and controlled as such.
- Customer performance of all parts of the organization will be measured on a common scale with a target of perfection as judged by the sigma metric.

Defects per million opportunities

This development of a common metric for quality adds considerable value to using Six Sigma as a quality standard. The technical definition of sigma as a metric has been explained above, but it is more often converted to a formal statement such as:

> the number of defects (experienced by customers) per million opportunities (for a defect to occur).

This in itself is much easier to understand, and much more practical in its application. There are weaknesses even in this definition, as will be outlined in the next section, but this is a powerful quality tool as a metric of customer experience of quality. Define carefully a *defect*, and the *opportunity* for defect, and this definition can place *any* process on a measurable scale, whether it is in manufacturing, service industry or life in general.

For example, let us return to our customer in the queue for the checkout at the supermarket. No one would deny that for this and any customer, a short queuing time is vital if the store is to be seen as providing a quality service. The definition of defect is clear – not reaching the head of the queue quickly enough – and there is one defect opportunity per customer (see Table 2.1). Whether you count two opportunities for defect if two people are queuing together is a moot point – especially if both are disappointed with the outcome. As a formal definition, defect opportunities should ideally be independent of each other, really matter to the customer, and increase numerically only with increased process complexity. Arriving at the definition of what constitutes a defect requires customer survey and analysis, as well as due consideration, and for the sake of this example we shall assume this to be two minutes, no more.

Measuring the sigma metric of this process is then straightforward. Count a number of customers, and see how many of these fail to reach the head of the queue in two minutes. Then convert this to a Defects Per Million Opportunities (DPMO) figure using the equation shown below, and use a standard DPMO-to-sigma conversion table:

$$\text{DPMO} = 1\,000\,000 \times (\text{Total Defects/Total Opportunities}) = 26\,000\,000/136 = 191\,176$$

Table 2.1 Defects and opportunities

Customers observed	136
Opportunities for defect per customer	1
Total opportunities for a defect	136
Customers failling to reach head of queue in two minutes	26
Defects measured	26

Conversion from DPMO to a process sigma metric generally requires the use of previously calculated tables. Table A.1 in the Appendix has been provided for this purpose, and it can been seen in this table that there is an entry for a DPMO of 192 200 against row 2.3 and column 0.07, relating to a sigma value of 2.37. This is the best match to 191 176, thus the example equates to a performance sigma metric of about 2.4 (there is often little point in expressing the process sigma metric to more than one decimal place). What this means in extrapolation is that for every one million customers who queue in this supermarket, about 190 000 are going to go away having experienced what *they* deem to be poor and unacceptable quality. These results are quite normal for processes, and indeed this was quite an acceptable level of quality in the past. The reality today is that such levels of performance are not tolerated. Should a rival supermarket change processes so that only 190 of their customers per million experience such a defect when queuing, customers would definitely notice. If queuing really is a quality issue and really does matter to customers, then many will change supermarkets as a result. Consumers can detect a difference of less than two sigma in the outcome of a process, which is similar to a one hundredfold reduction in defects.

By using DPMO as a common measure of quality, it is further possible to combine entirely different processes into one common sigma metric simply by taking all possible defects and all possible defect opportunities across the process. Indeed, this is often how businesses bring all their core process sigma metrics into one single figure. It does involve a certain amount of sleight of hand, and requires a balanced overview of what really matters to customers. If successfully achieved, the gains are that someone, for example in the manufacturing department, can talk about quality on the same scale as someone else from the customer accounts department, and the customer-value and performance of both processes can be compared.

STATISTICAL PRIMER

It is not the intention of this book to attempt to reproduce any standard statistics text, as most well-stocked bookshops will have many excellent volumes from which to choose. Rather, the aim is to draw together in one place the majority of the essential statistical issues that either directly affect or are strategically involved with Six Sigma as a quality methodology.

Two types of statistics

Statistics can be broadly divided into two areas: *descriptive* statistics and *inferential* statistics. The first area is concerned with measuring, organizing and summarizing information of particular interest. This includes such matters as sampling, tabulation, data-manipulation and graphical presentation, and most of the tools used here will be comfortably familiar to anyone in an organization. The issues for this area of statistics are: identifying exactly what information is required, ensuring that it is collected in an appropriate manner, and then presenting it in such a way as not to distort or misrepresent. Descriptive statistics are a means to inform and perhaps add some value to a point in question. Misuse of statistics has in the past led to considerable suspicion, and care must be exercised lest mistrust of the results is the only outcome.

Inferential statistics is relatively recent; most statistical methods used by statisticians today are no more than a hundred years old. This area of statistics includes several techniques for drawing conclusions about a population (and measuring their reliability) based on information obtained from a sample of the population. This is certainly a more difficult area, and will most likely need expert input. However, the use of such methods is highly unlikely during the early stages of a quality initiative, and is also more likely to be limited to manufacturing processes. Advanced statistical methods are very tricky to apply to the often unstable and fuzzy service transaction process, so they can rarely be relied upon if used in isolation in such a project. Inferential statistics can add some value to certain projects, and the fact that non-manufacturing is so difficult to deal with is no reason to abandon statistics or Six Sigma in this area.

Statistical software

Collecting and analysing data is a major part of Six Sigma projects, and it is vital to use appropriate software. The *Microsoft Office* spreadsheet program, *Excel*, is one of a number of excellent tools that can be used to gather and manipulate data. It does have a 'data analysis add-in', which provides some of the statistical tools required, but there are other packages specifically designed to perform advanced statistics and data-presentation. *Minitab* is a very comprehensive software tool that goes beyond a simple spreadsheet, and in particular it is very good at producing control charts and histograms, and it can perform advanced data-manipulation. Experience has shown that in the hands of well-trained and experienced staff, a combination of database, spreadsheet and statistical software can quickly deliver accurate information and conclusions to assist quality teams. Non-manufacturing organizations are unlikely to be familiar with the use of any statistical methods, and it can take quite some time to acquire and develop the necessary skills and expertise in this area.

Sampling techniques

Statistical methods work better when there exists an abundance of first-class quality data. Analysing just four or five data points of dubious value for a trend or pattern is simply not helpful, but the converse problem that a large quantity of data brings is that it is usually not possible to deal with it all. No marketing or survey company would question every single voting adult, simply because such a census would take far too long. The secret is to take a *sample* of the entire set of data (population), but this requires some care. Two factors matter in a sample: how many data points are collected, and how they are chosen. Without going into complicated mathematics, a good rule of thumb is 30 data points as a minimum, or 10–15 per cent of the population, whichever is larger. Puritans of statistical methods may disagree with this point, but it is the practical and sensible application of statistics that is of interest, particularly in non-manufacturing organizations, where most people who will be involved with such work are unfamiliar with these concepts. Where few understand the complex underlying principles, one or two rules of thumb will ensure that the most drastic mistakes are avoided, and too few data points in a sample is a common error in judgement.

Simple random sampling is the easiest to perform; other types include systematic random sampling, cluster sampling, stratified sampling and multi-stage sampling. In simple random sampling, each item in the entire population must have an equal chance of being selected. For example, decide perhaps to take 20 per cent of all data – that is, 1 in every 5. Starting with item 1 and then picking every fifth item is not a random sample, since items 2, 3, 4 and so on will never be chosen. It is necessary to start the selection at a *random* number between 1 and 5, and then to take every fifth data point, and in this way each point could possibly have been included.

Descriptive statistics

The information collected for analysis is commonly referred to as *variable data*; it is data from a characteristic that varies from one item to another. The 'rule of two' seems to apply throughout statistics, as there are two types of variable data, qualitative and quantitative, and quantitative data is further divided into discrete and continuous.

If the data measured falls into one of a number of non-numerical 'baskets', such as male or female, child or adult, hot or cold, then it is *qualitative*. Such data is of considerable use to Six Sigma initiatives, in some cases it may be all that is available, and it is also much easier to collect from surveys, to measure, analyse and display. However, it suffers from considerable drawbacks where detailed statistical analysis is required, and every attempt should be made to avoid collecting and working with qualitative data alone.

Quantitative data is numerical, such as age, weight, length, time and counts of things. To differentiate between discrete and continuous data can be difficult, as both time and money are continuous data, even if we normally choose to measure money in discrete amounts. The fundamental difference is that any continuous data measure can, in theory, be sub-divided into smaller and smaller units *ad infinitum*, whereas discrete data units cannot. Money may be measured in cents, for example, but in theory governments could issue half cents, then quarter cents, and so on. A count of the number of persons in a household is discrete, as there is no such thing as a half or quarter person. Again, the value of continuous data to inferential statistical analysis far outweighs that of discrete data, and the real problem is that it is far too easy to turn good continuous data into poor discrete data by sloppy collection processes.

Once data has been collected, it can be analysed and displayed in a variety of ways. Pictures always have far more impact than tables of data, and diagrams such as bar charts, time series plots and pie charts are easy to produce. The example in Figure 2.4 clearly (but fictitiously) shows the importance of existing loyalty-card customers.

Frequency distributions

Collecting a reasonable quantity of continuous data allows a frequency table to be constructed. This is normally done automatically when plotting a histogram, but the practical tasks involved are quite simple. The maximum value and the minimum value from the data set define the range of the data, and this range can then be divided into a number of 'bins'. Usually, these are of equal

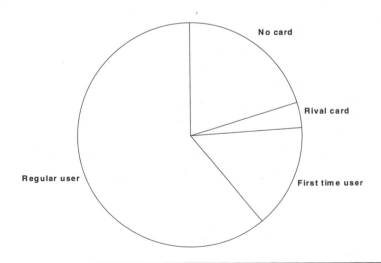

Figure 2.4 Example of a pie chart

size and consecutive, and are then used to count how many of the collected data points fall into each bin. This will then show the frequency with which data occurs within each data bin. Plotting a vertical bar whose height represents the number of items for that bin is then straightforward. (In fact, it is the *area* of the bar that represents the number of data points in each bin, but since for the most part the bins are constructed of equal size, this is of little consequence.)

It should be emphasized that if the data bins are continuous and consecutive, the chart produced is a histogram. If the bins are of discrete data and not numerically connected, as in the pie chart shown in Figure 2.4, the chart produced is a bar chart. To consider an example from real life, it may be of interest to produce a frequency distribution of the heights of all six-year-old children in London. Choosing children aged between six years and six years and 364 days easily avoids any issues resulting from the random growth changes at adolescence which would result in a more complex pattern. Taking all such children in London would further ensure that the sample size or census was large enough (probably about 100 000) to arrive at an excellent result, even if this would be somewhat impractical! The range of the distribution would go from the shortest child to the tallest, and for simplicity each data 'bin' range could cover exactly 1 centimetre or even just 1 millimetre as an incremental step. By drawing a line along the ground and marking off equal spaces, each height range bin could be provided with a corresponding space along the line. Each child could then be 'pigeonholed' into the corresponding bin, according to their height. If each child then stands at the line and similar-height children form an equally spaced queue extending away from the line, the view from above would show a neat frequency distribution of the height of six-year-old children.

Frequency distributions are of considerable interest and much practical use, and in statistics it is found that almost every set of data will follow, in general, one of only a few unique patterns. Over the past few hundred years, all naturally occurring frequency distributions have been identified and studied. The simplest of these is the *uniform distribution* (see Figure 2.5), which is actually quite unnatural and occurs only infrequently. It is this distribution that describes the outcome of any well-run lottery, in that every number occurs with exactly the same frequency. This is one of the endearing principles of frequency distributions. If we measure something of interest over a period of time and plot the distribution, the historical frequency distribution can then be used as a probability distribution to predict what will happen in the future. In this case, the height of line, which has been plotted from the historical observation of frequency, serves as a guide to the future probability of observation.

Of all possible distribution types, only three are of any real interest within Six Sigma. The *binomial distribution* (see Figure 2.6) is a measure of outcome from discrete random variables, and applies to events such as the outcome of repeatedly tossing a coin, or a task where the outcome is either pass or fail, as may be found in many manufacturing processes. To help understand the binomial distribution, think of ten pieces of wood of the same length (like rulers), all joined by hinges at each end, and lying flat on a table. Each piece can take one of two discrete positions, folded either left or right. If one end of this chain is connected to a fixed point, the other end will end up a certain distance away, the value of which depends on how many of the links fall to the left and how many to the right. Only if every link falls the same way will the end of the chain be 10 units away, but there many ways in which links can be folded, and indeed the most common outcome will be that the chain ends back where it started.

The *Poisson distribution* was first described by Simeon Poisson, a French mathematician and physicist who conducted his principal work by recording the intervals between incidents of death

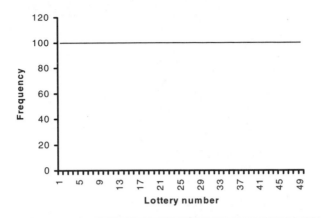

Figure 2.5 The uniform distribution

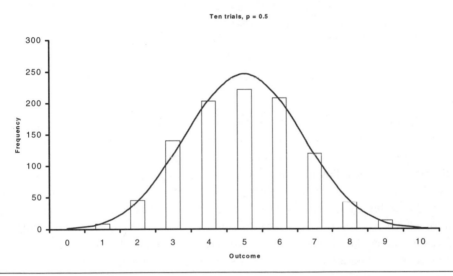

Figure 2.6 The binomial distribution

in Napoleon's army during peacetime (the most common causes being death from mule kicks – dangerous things, mules and donkeys). This again discrete distribution models the frequency with which independent events occur during a given period, such as the number of incoming telephone calls per minute. While important in its own area, the Poisson distribution is principally restricted to random and independent events occurring during an interval of time, and would be used to model such things as the demand for services from a queue. Figure 2.7 shows the distribution for telephone calls arriving at a switchboard or call centre, where the overall average rate of calls is an unlikely but steady eight per minute during the day. Even if in any one minute the average call rate is eight calls, there will be some minutes where more or fewer calls are received. Here it can be seen that over 1000 minutes, it would be expected that 85 one-minute intervals would see only 5 calls, and 20 separate one-minute intervals would see as many as 14 calls. Such analysis allows for predictive modelling and the efficient design of processes to be capable of meeting the greatest expected demand without suffering resource overload.

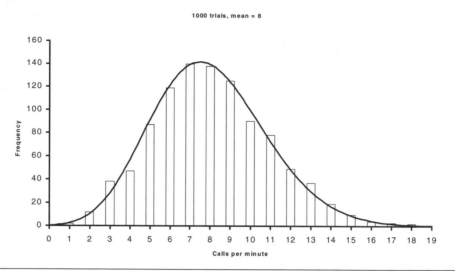

Figure 2.7 The Poisson distribution

The normal distribution

The binomial distribution considers discrete random events, such as the results of tossing a coin a number of times. In the real, natural world, such events are rare, and outcomes are more usually the results of the interaction of a number of randomly occurring and independent factors with continuous, not discrete, outcomes. Rather than a number of fixed lengths of wood hinged so as to fall either left or right, consider a number of elastic bands, each taking a different random length. The resulting distribution has many similarities to the binomial distribution, but is much more likely to be found in real life. Certainly, the frequency distribution of the height of all six-year-old children in London imagined earlier would be a classical normal distribution, as height is a continuous variable. However, under certain conditions, it is even possible to approximate a given binomial distribution to an equivalent normal distribution, and Figure 2.6 does look remarkably similar to Figure 2.2.

Consider, for example, an apple tree in an orchard. The genetics of the tree dictate that each apple should be of a certain identical size and weight. However, pick all the apples on a large tree and plot the distribution of the resulting weights of each apple, and the result would be a picture resembling that of the normal distribution. For each apple, the actual weight is an ideal outcome interfered with by many conflicting factors that each operate randomly and independently. The age of the tree and its size, number of apples on the tree, position of each apple, weather and soil conditions, pests and diseases all affect the final outcome for any particular apple. It is this fundamental and naturally occurring random variation which produces the effect we see in the normal distribution – and this is why it is of such interest to Six Sigma quality. Almost every single process exhibits normal distribution variation, or something that closely approximates to it.

The current understanding of the normal distribution is principally due to the work of Carl Gauss, a noted German scientist and mathematician of the late eighteenth and early nineteenth centuries. Called the Gaussian distribution in his honour, the term *normal distribution* is more often used, reflecting as it does the fact that this distribution describes almost anything normally encountered in the real world.

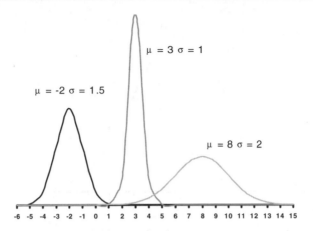

$\mu = 3\ \sigma = 1$

$\mu = -2\ \sigma = 1.5$

$\mu = 8\ \sigma = 2$

-6 -5 -4 -3 -2 -1 0 1 2 3 4 5 6 7 8 9 10 11 12 13 14 15

Figure 2.8 Three examples of a normal distribution

Figure 2.8 shows three examples of a normal distribution, plotted on the same axis. There are very many different instances of this shape, but each can be classified by two variables: the *mean* (average), and the *standard deviation* (or sigma) of the curve. It is not necessary to plot a series of numbers graphically like this to be able to find the values of the mean and sigma, as the mean is simply the mathematical average, and standard deviation for a set of numbers can be easily calculated on any modern scientific calculator. However, the graphical representation does have the advantage of clearly showing how standard deviation relates to the Six Sigma metric.

Taking the right-hand curve of the three examples, it might be of interest to learn how much of this curve lies to the left or right of a point at, for example, 11 on the horizontal axis. This information would show both the historical and the future probability of an outcome being either above or below the value 11. Probability outcome is related to the area under the curve, but because of the mathematical complexity of the normal curve, there exists no simple formula to calculate the area under part of the normal curve. Rather, such values are found by calculating and summing a complex series of numbers, and it is necessary to use either a computer or look-up tables to obtain this information.

The normal distribution is so important that one particular standardized curve has been defined. Called the *standard normal curve*, it has a mean of zero and a value of sigma of 1, and encloses an area under the entire curve of exactly 1. From this standard curve, pre-calculated tables can be used to find the properties of z, a variable often used to measure a fractional part of the area under the curve. On the standard normal curve, z is simply taken as the number on the horizontal axis. However, from any normal distribution, the z value for any point x on the curve is found by using the formula:

$$z = (x - \mu)/\sigma$$

What this allows is that for any given set of data which approximates to the normal distribution, having calculated a value for the mean and for the standard deviation, it is possible to calculate the value of z for any particular data point. From this value of z, the area under the curve either side of the point x is found by reference to tables for the area under the standard normal curve. As the standard normal curve is so very important, such tables for the 'area under the curve to the left of a specified value of z' are reproduced in almost every statistical textbook and reference, and the

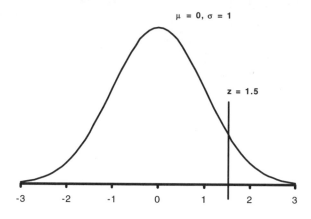

Figure 2.9   The standard normal curve

reader will have no real difficulty in locating such tables. A word of caution: it must be noted that z does not relate directly to the Six Sigma process sigma metric, as will be shown in the next section. Table A.1 in the Appendix includes an adjustment between z and process sigma.

In the example in Figure 2.8, where the interest was to find the proportion of the curve to the right of the value 11, x is 11, μ is 8 and σ is 2, which means that z = 1.5. On the standard normal curve (see Figure 2.9), the area to the left of x where z = 1.5 is 0.9332, and to the right it is 1 − 0.9332, or 0.0668 (as found from tables). This value applies also to the example, in that the area under the curve to the left of 11 is also 0.9332 of the whole area, or close to 93 per cent.

Three sigma and Six Sigma

It can be seen from the diagram of the standard normal curve that almost the entire visible area under the curve lies within three standard deviations either side of the mean, even though the curve actually goes on and on, never quite reaching the horizontal axis. Historically, this has had an impact in two important ways. Firstly, as calculating the area under the curve had to be done by hand and was then published in tables, results tended to be limited to four significant figures. Even today, with sophisticated computers available to perform such calculations, tables for the area under the standard normal curve often stop at 3.9 with a note that 'areas are 1.0000 to four figures'. Secondly, it is a practical limit, since the area between −3 and +3 is 99.74 per cent of the entire curve, very close to 100 per cent. Back in the 1920s, it was realized that as long as a process was set up in such as way as there were three standard deviations between the mean and the specified process limits, for all *practical* purposes all output would fall inside these limits. This, then, is the historical basis of Statistical Process Control and quality. It also served as the basis for most consumer-based manufacture, since a clothing manufacturer producing coats for six-year-old children can satisfy almost every child by providing for a range of heights just three standard deviations either side of the mean. This would fail to encompass only 260 out of our 100 000 children in the earlier example. In fact, most manufacturers only provide for a range of just one or two standard deviations either side of the mean, which still account for between 70 and 95 per cent of all sizes.

So why is it necessary today to extend this limit from three to six standard deviations or sigma?

There are two reasons. Firstly, three sigma still leaves an error that has now become unacceptable to modern manufacturing industry, and secondly, the idea that processes at three sigma capability only fail 0.26 per cent of the time is seen in general practice to be a myth. Early work with processes in manufacturing showed that over a period of time, output from a process would change. Either the mean of the distribution would shift sideways a little, or the standard deviation would change and the curve would begin to spread a little. The consequence of this is that more and more of the tails of the curve extend beyond the expected three sigma limits. It has become accepted practice (by some, but not all) to devalue the three sigma ideal by 1.5 sigma, which is perhaps an arbitrary but realistic figure backed by years of empirical experience in manufacturing. Any process set up to operate at a three sigma performance in the *short term* is accepted as probably only delivering a one-and-a-half sigma output over the *long term*, and hence long-term sigma is 1.5 less than short-term sigma. To state that a process has the capability of operating at three sigma performance is actually to accept a failure rate equal to the area under the standard normal curve outside of 1.5 standard deviations of the mean, or close to 7 per cent.

Six Sigma is no exception to this rule, and close examination of z tables (which go beyond 3.9) will show that for an expected performance of Six Sigma for the short term, the Six Sigma defect rate is in fact equal to that at four-and-a-half sigma for the long term.

This difference is rarely explained and justified, and several commentators have expressed an opinion that because of this alone, Six Sigma is a confidence trick and almost not to be trusted. This is simply not the case – if anything, it is the unspoken three sigma standard that has for over sixty years been the confidence trick. What is being discussed here is process capability, and not really error rate. Certainly, a 'three sigma-capable' process can deliver at three sigma performance, but over time it will tend to deliver only a one-and-a-half sigma performance, equivalent to 66 800 defects per million. Assuming a perfect world, a three sigma process delivers just that, but this world is not perfect. Six Sigma has aimed higher, and has effectively doubled the ideal process capability from three to six. Although a process may achieve Six Sigma performance in the short term, it is again accepted that in the long term, this might fall to four-and-a-half sigma, and so error rates for Six Sigma are quoted at 4.5 sigma levels, equivalent to under 4 parts per million. Looked at from this perspective, quality is currently at a one-and-a-half sigma performance, and is now aiming for four-and-a-half sigma performance, which makes the jump sound even more impressive than from three to six.

All of this is really about process capability, which is often far removed from customer satisfaction. Because of the conceptual difficulties in understanding the above, and particularly the 1.5 sigma shift, Six Sigma is too often talked about as defects per million opportunities. Experience of consumers today would point to the fact that a 10 per cent failure rate in meeting their expectations is certainly not unknown. What is called 'three sigma' is exactly what is found when any organization first undertakes the Six Sigma quality initiative. What is called 'Six Sigma', however it is measured, guarantees to always deliver no more than 4 defects in a million, even when the 1.5 sigma shift has been applied.

Figure 2.10 shows a number of normal curve distributions between two sets of specified process limits. The limits at +3 and −3 equate to customer requirements for this process. The first distribution is centred between the limits (mean of zero), and has a standard deviation value of 1. As the distance between the mean and both limits is three times the standard deviation, this process has a process sigma metric of three. This is a typical three sigma-capable process, and the amount of the curve that falls outside both limits is about 0.25 per cent.

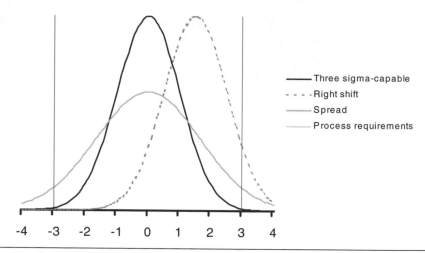

Figure 2.10 The effect of shift and spread on performance sigma

The right-hand curve has exactly the same standard deviation value of 1, but the mean has shifted to the right by about 1.5, and there is now much more of the curve outside the process limits, in fact approximately 7 per cent. The third curve remains centred, but has a larger value of standard deviation, here close to 1.65 – this is the *curve* sigma metric. The distance between the centre of this curve and the process limits can only be expressed as a smaller number of standard deviations, in this case a distance of 3 divided by 1.65 which is close to 1.8 sigma – this is the *process* sigma metric, and the area outside of the limits is again approximately 7 per cent. A confusing difference: the *curve* has a standard deviation or sigma which is a measure of how 'fat' the curve is (1.65), and the *process* has a sigma metric (1.8) which is a measure of how many standard deviations (sigma) fit between the mean and the given process limits. To avoid confusion, it is perhaps better to call the curve sigma metric by the full title of *standard deviation*, rather than sigma!

These curves may also help explain the very confusing difference between short-term and long-term process sigma. Motorola was first to define the way in which Six Sigma values are measured, and providing everyone sticks to this approach, there is no real reason to change, even if it is almost incomprehensible and generates considerable debate.

If the measurable outcome of a given process changes over time due to shift and spread, then we can have no idea when we first measure it how well it will really perform over time. Assume that a process has been improved upon and initially set up to deliver at three sigma in the short term, which will be similar to the 'thin' centred curve in Figure 2.10. Although there are three standard deviations between mean and limits, over the long term the performance is expected to degrade and deliver only a one-and-a-half sigma performance, which has an error rate of about 7 per cent. Thus, the measured and short-term process sigma is actually associated with a long-term performance of 93 per cent success. If the same process is measured several months later, performance may have degraded to that of the 'fat' curve in Figure 2.10, and a measure of error will show the expected 7 per cent failure. However, it can be assumed that over time, the process will return back to the initial 'best situation', where there are three standard deviations between mean and limits.

Conversely, if a non-improved process is visited for the first time and measured as having a 7 per cent failure rate, then in reality it will be performing as the 'fat' curve. The process performance is still stated to be three sigma in the short term, as it is expected that this is the best possible scenario from which degradation has lowered the performance, and to which it should (or could) return. If the process is 'smartened up', then it should indeed return to being like the 'thin' curve, and exhibit three standard deviations between mean and limits. It is likely to revert in time to the lower performance, so a process capability of three sigma is again associated with a worst long-term performance of 1.5 standard deviations.

To attempt to summarize and simplify: specifying that a process has a performance of three sigma is to say that at its best it will be *capable* of being three standard deviations between mean and limits for the short term, but in reality deliver a worst-case *performance* of only 1.5 standard deviations (and 7 per cent error) in the long term. Over time, all situations between the best capability and worst performance should be seen. The real difficulty comes if a process is measured at 7 per cent error rate, claimed to be three sigma-capable, but does not naturally change or improve over the long term and still remains in this state. It is even more problematic if the process actually degrades and shifts even further, which implies that the measured 7 per cent error was the best case, not the worst. If the 'fat' curve is always seen, then the assumed short-term and long-term performance difference does not apply, and the process performance will have to be stated as being the lower value of the two. In such cases, three sigma is in reality only one-and-a-half sigma.

More formally, it is the difference between 'short-term' and 'long-term' that guides the appropriate application of the 1.5 sigma shift. Data collected in the short term will show a process capability that should be (1.5 sigma) better than the process performance from data collected over the long term. For manufacturing processes, short-term will be one machine, one operator, one shift, one component, one process step, and so on. Service processes are inherently more complex and rarely allow the collection of short-term data: here, data collected will always be long-term, and will cover many operations, many people, many shifts, many days, many process stages, and so on. Such long-term data will provide the long-term sigma metric for process performance. Adding 1.5 will then turn this into the short-term sigma metric for process capability.

If all of this remains totally incomprehensible to the reader, then the best approach is to keep to the concept of defect count, and use the accepted (and shifted) tables as the adopted standard. Indeed, there may be no alternative in the case of many service processes.

Figure 2.11 shows the visible difference between a three sigma-capable process (the 'fat' curve) and a Six Sigma-capable process (the 'thin' curve), shown against identical process limits. The aim of Six Sigma quality is to ensure that the outcome of each process sits within customer limits like this: the mean of the outcome is centred between the limits, and the standard deviation of the outcome is so small that customers experience defective outcomes only very rarely. Even when failing to make allowance on such a diagram for the 1.5 sigma shift, the difference between three and six sigma is still better than 2000 defects for every million opportunities, but this is only half the story. Not only does a Six Sigma approach reduce the likelihood of an outcome falling outside the process limits, but it also provides more room for manoeuvre, in that the distribution curve can move or spread slightly without having much impact on the defect rate. The three sigma curve is not so tolerant.

Calculating process sigma: An example

Bringing together all the above, it is now possible to demonstrate an example of a full calculation of process sigma. In this instance, we have a process with a mean of 100 and a standard deviation

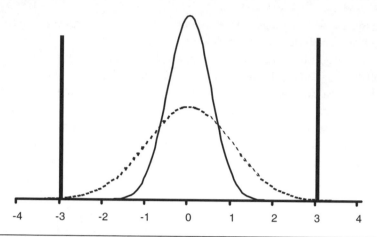

Figure 2.11 The visible difference between three and six sigma

of only 4. From customer survey, it has been decided that the upper and lower acceptable limits for this process are 106 and 92. There are two possible ways to arrive at the process sigma metric for this particular case. The first is the full calculation method (see Figure 2.12):

1 Determine the normal distribution, its mean, standard deviation, and upper and lower customer limits.
2 Convert each customer limit to a z value, and then look up the corresponding areas under the standard normal curve from tables.
3 Work out the area between the limits, and then convert this back to a single right-hand tail, and the corresponding value of z.
4 Add 1.5 to this value of z to arrive at the short-term process sigma, which is 2.84.

The method using defects is by far the simpler. By counting both total opportunities and total defects observed, the defects per million opportunities can be converted to a process sigma value from a pre-calculated table of such values. In this example, for every million outcomes, 22 800

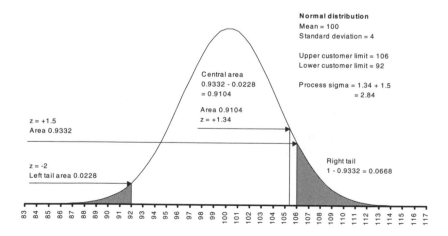

Figure 2.12 Calculating process sigma directly from the normal distribution

would be a defect from the left-hand tail, and 66 800 a defect from the right-hand tail. This is in total 89 600 defects. Of course, it is very unlikely that any process would deliver a million outcomes in a short space of time, so it may be that 90 defects are seen in 1000, or 45 defects in 500 outcomes, or nine defects in 100 outcomes. Looking up a DPMO of 89 600 in a DPMO-to-sigma table (see Appendix, Table A.1) shows the short-term process sigma to be about 2.84 (equivalent to 90 120 defects, which is close enough).

It must be stressed that the DPMO method is approximate and becomes unreliable when the absolute defect count is small (less than about five). At a process performance of four sigma, the defect rate is about 1 per cent. In manufacturing, where thousands of widgets are coming off the production line per hour, it does not take long to count the defects. In a service industry with perhaps only ten customers per month, the DPMO method can be wholly inappropriate. Binomial distributions have many similarities to normal distributions, and it is standard practice to apply the rules for the area under the curve of a normal distribution to similar binomial distributions. Although this does not work for all cases, in situations where discrete, not continuous, data is being used for Six Sigma work, the DPMO count method for calculating the process sigma metric is an acceptable approximation. Again, at the extremes with very large or very small error rates, the approximations no longer hold, and more formal (and complex) approaches should be applied. In practice, where error rates are very large the correct application of statistics is almost pointless, and more often than not confuses both issues and people. When operating at a process performance of four sigma or better, there is no room for haphazard and slapdash methods, and more care will be required, both in the theory and execution of the statistics involved. Here, *confidence intervals* begin to play an important role in deciding how much confidence can be ascribed to the calculated result (see 'Inferential statistics' below).

Non-normal distributions

The classic textbook diagram is one matter, but data from real life seldom looks so neat and tidy. The fundamental cause of the normal distribution is the naturally occurring variation in the real world. Cutting lengths of steel rod will always produce a slightly different length every time, because of unavoidable variations in measured length, the size of the rod, where the saw blade falls, and so on. Over and above these factors occur non-natural variations, due to such things as different shift operators and cutting procedures, changes in the setting of the machine, daily and seasonal temperature variations in the workshop, and so on. Most manufacturing processes are set up specifically to eliminate such non-natural variation, indeed the principal aim of mass-manufacturing is to set up processes to deliver identical items time after time, regardless of who operates the machine or what time of day it is. Service industry is rather different, as processes are not always fully documented, let alone controlled. It is not uncommon in such processes to find that the non-natural variation entirely overshadows the natural. When this is the case, the shape of the plotted distribution will not look like the normal curve. The underlying behaviour is that of the normal distribution, but the data has been transformed or skewed in some way. It is good practice when dealing with such data to first remove excessively out-of-pattern data, to test for 'normality' (adherence to an ideal normal distribution), and then transform the data back to a normal curve. The 'Box-Cox' transform available in some statistical packages can easily identify and apply the necessary transform to correct the skewed data. This is particularly important when dealing with service process outcomes that are related to time duration. Often, the outcome has become very heavily skewed to the left with a long tail to the right, as it is always easy to delay a process, but never possible to cheat time.

Practical common sense is also very useful, as other distortions of the curve such as multi-mode distributions (where two or more normal curves overlap each other) require human interpretation as much as methodical data analysis to understand. The theory of the normal curve states that it continues left and right, never quite reaching zero, and in practice this can lead to absurd inferences. Plotting the height of every adult in the UK would produce a normal distribution. The mean is the average height for all adults, probably 1.7 metres or so. The standard deviation would be about 0.07 metres, so almost all the population would be between 1.5 and 1.9 metres tall, that is, plus or minus three standard deviations on either side of the mean. However, the distribution implies that 3 people in every million are taller than 2 metres, and 1 in every thousand million is taller than 2.1 metres. This does happen, but there has to be an upper practical limit. There are no apples the size of houses, and tidal waves do not reach the size of the planet, simply because apples physically stop growing after a certain size and there is a physical limit to the amount of water in the oceans. This is very evident in processes where practical stops are put in place to prevent out-of-range output. Indeed, the historical contribution of quality assurance has been to reject such output and send it either to the scrap heap or to be reworked, and it may be necessary to dig deeper in such cases to locate missing parts of a distribution.

Inferential statistics

Often, it is just not possible to measure the entire population of items of interest. Only by measuring every single outcome can the true and accurate mean and standard deviation be found, but it is possible to infer behaviours of the whole population by considering known facts about a sampled part.

Inferential statistics covers such areas as *confidence intervals, hypothesis tests* and *regression and correlation analysis*, detailed discussion of which is beyond the scope of this book. If there is any part of Six Sigma as a methodology that needs to be set aside for specialists, then this is certainly a prime candidate. Few people have either the interest or ability to perform statistical hypothesis tests, and such expertise is often simply not available in non-manufacturing organizations. As will be shown later, implementing Six Sigma in a company requires tiers of individuals with different skills, each with a particular role to play in leading, running and supporting quality improvement. For non-manufacturing organizations, it is appropriate to specifically enhance the position of the expert in Six Sigma quality, usually known as a Master Black Belt. Such people benefit from advanced statistical training and practical experience gained from working with the low-grade data associated with service processes (often material that most statisticians would not even consider worth a second look). Such experienced and trained people provide essential, practical and realistic statistical analysis support and guidance as and when it is required.

SIX SIGMA IN MANUFACTURING

The driving force for the new standard that is Six Sigma quality has come from within global manufacturing, where the scale and type of production implies that 99 per cent product quality is no longer good enough. Back in the 1920s, it is likely that production processes had considerably more tolerance to error, and the cost of a defect would be small. Large-scale mass production was limited principally to motor car manufacture, where Ford and other companies were applying economies of scale to the production line. The way cars were put together implied that if the glass for a windscreen did not quite fit, then small adjustments might be made on the spot, or the glass would be scrapped. Either way, the customer paid. Even as late as the early 1980s, such vehicles as the Land Rover (Series Three) showed how much 'give and take' had been built in to the original design, which in parts dated back to before the Second World War. It had been shown many times that an early Land Rover could be maintained in the middle of a desert with only the most rudimentary of tools and skills, but the overall performance of such machines was poor. The engine piston rings allowed copious amounts of sump oil to leak into the upper cylinder, but the result was ease of production and maintenance – it had worked for almost fifty years, so why change?

The UK and USA have a long tradition of innovation and design, but 'necessity is the mother of invention', and without the necessity, it is far too easy not to invent and to remain with the *status quo*. Japanese industry, on the other hand, had nothing to lose, and had no difficulty in obtaining competitors' cars, taking them apart piece by piece, and then improving on everything it found. There was a time when many Japanese competitors knew more about a car than the original manufacturer did.

The necessity for the Japanese industry was to break into foreign markets, in which they were never leaders, had no competitive edge and little experience. How could this possibly be achieved? The answer is simple: be much cheaper than anyone else. Cost is a strong determining factor, but it is not everything, and if lowering cost means lowering quality, as it usually had in the past, then Japanese manufacturers soon gained a reputation for low-cost and low-quality products. The aim therefore had to be to produce something of equal or better *worth*, at a lower cost, and this meant eliminating waste and every unnecessary expense. By distilling the very essence of what customers wanted, and then redesigning both processes and products to deliver this at zero waste, the Japanese destroyed for ever the far too comfortable relationship between product cost and quality.

In manufacturing today, it is no longer possible to pass the expense involved in generating good quality back to the customer, since someone else in the world will soon find a way of delivering similar quality without the associated costs. Historically, improved quality meant greater quality assurance, where additional expenditure was involved with testing and rejecting products after manufacture. The quality concept today is that better quality actually saves money. None of this is particularly new, but manufacturing has been for too long obsessed with *product* quality, and not *customer* quality. Only by looking beyond product specifications and quality assurance can manufacturing see that excellent quality comes with total customer satisfaction, and it is only by applying both the metric and philosophy of Six Sigma that this can be achieved. Manufacturing has employed several quality methodologies to help improve product quality and reduce costs, but Six Sigma goes beyond this and brings a new emphasis to three essential areas:

- customer requirements;
- process improvement for defect-reduction;
- Total Quality Management involving all employees.

The 'cost of (ensuring) quality' is a real limiting factor in what can be practically achieved in terms of delivered excellence to the customer. The practical steps involved in guaranteeing product or service quality do inevitably require an associated cost and overhead, which has traditionally been balanced against the reduction in real costs associated with failures and rework from poor quality. Figure 2.13 shows the equilibrium point at which the cost of delivering good quality balances

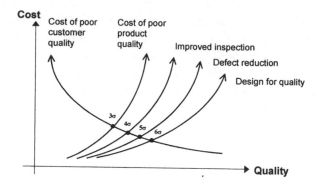

Figure 2.13   A move towards Six Sigma quality drives down cost

against the cost suffered as a result of poor quality, and also shows how this point can be shifted. Various levels of attainment have been associated with companies which increase quality through better inspection, quality assurance, better design and operation of processes, and the ultimate goal of 'zero' defects. Such levels can be tied loosely to Six Sigma process metrics of three, four, five and six sigma, and the various stages in implementing Six Sigma quality. The important point to note is that only by removing error, failure and rework rather than increasing inspection and quality assurance can the cost equilibrium point be shifted towards a better level of performance.

The dramatic impact that Six Sigma quality can have on modern manufacturing is shown in Table 2.2. Today, motor cars and computers are constructed from many more component parts than similar items of twenty years ago. Each stage of the process adds a new part or step, and each

Table 2.2   Comparison of multi-stage final yield

	3 sigma	4 sigma	5 sigma	6 sigma
Single-step yield	93%	99%	99.977%	99.9997%
Part complexity			*Final yield (%)*	
1	93	99	100.0	100.00
2	87	99	100.0	100.00
3	81	98	99.9	100.00
4	76	98	99.9	100.00
5	71	97	99.9	100.00
6	66	96	99.9	100.00
7	62	96	99.8	100.00
8	58	95	99.8	100.00
9	54	95	99.8	100.00
10	50	94	99.8	100.00
20	25	88	99.5	99.99
30	13	83	99.3	99.99
40	6	78	99.1	99.99
50	3	73	98.9	99.99
100	0	54	97.7	99.97

of these steps will have a proportion of rejects. The issue is not the successful yield at each stage, but the overall successful yield after 10, 20 or 100 steps. At three sigma performance, each step will pass on to the next only 93 per cent without failure, and after two successive steps the error is compounded. For a 100-step process, no single entity can be produced without some necessary rework. Even at four sigma, with only a 1 per cent failure rate at each step, a 100-step process will require rework on almost half of the output, and with manufacturing becoming increasingly complex, rework is sometimes just not possible. With very large-scale computer microprocessors, where an error at step 13 may not be detectable until step 74, even the difference between five and six sigma can improve yield by over 2 per cent. It should also be noted that the improvement in final quality yield against the single part error rate is dramatic. Even with only a ten-component part complexity, just moving from three sigma performance to four sigma performance at each step increases the zero-failure output by 90 per cent.

STATISTICAL PROCESS CONTROL

Manufacturing and production procedures have long enjoyed the advantages that statistics brings to the task of controlling any process. If the essential aim is to produce all output within a certain range, then once set in motion, every production process needs continuous monitoring to ensure that all output is indeed within this range.

For a company producing, for example, bars of chocolate, the weight of each bar is of paramount importance. One possibility is to weigh every bar, but if production is in the millions, this is both impractical and expensive. The answer is to monitor a sample, and to deduce using statistical methods the behaviour of the entire population.

Products with a stated weight of 125 grams (about 4 oz) must (by consumer protection law) either have not less than 125 grams, or an average of 125 grams within a given tolerance. (UK legislation changed a number of years ago after entry into the Common Market, and manufacturers can now base measurements on averages.) From the manufacturer's point of view, any more than 125 grams is product that could go in another package, so both the upper and lower customer limits are as close to 125 as is possible. The distribution of all possible outputs is again a normal curve with a measurable mean and standard deviation, and statistical methods enable quality control departments to ascertain the performance of the process, and to deduce how much of the production is probably falling outside the control limits.

Statistical monitoring can be further extended by using *Shewhart control charts* (see Figure 6.2) to indicate any long-term changes in the process. A control chart is a statistical tool designed to monitor measurements such as process metrics over a period of time, and to make it easier to separate critical and unexpected changes from the normally expected random variation. Coupled with appropriate action plans, this allows plant controllers responsible for output quality to respond to changes *before* they become critical. Over a period of time, the key mechanism that ensures exactly 125 grams of product is dispensed will change its performance. Natural variation is unavoidable, but controllable within limits. Special causes of variation, like a shifting or failing part in a machine or a change to the product mixture which affects viscosity and hence dispense rate, must be detected and action taken rapidly.

This is predominantly a practical extension of the same theory upon which the Six Sigma concept and metric are founded. Six Sigma therefore embodies much of what was already well practised in the field of Statistical Process Control.

TOTAL QUALITY MANAGEMENT

Many attempts to introduce better-quality practices have used the principles found within Total Quality Management (TQM), which aims to achieve practically zero defects, reduce variation in output, and innovate new procedures and processes in both manufacturing and service industries. The methods and principles of TQM have been shown to work satisfactorily or better in many situations, and there is every reason to use the tools and techniques that have evolved. TQM asserts the importance of a process chain, in which everyone is both a supplier and a customer, and the value of internal customers within this chain. TQM also recognizes the importance of every employee, and the cultural barriers that prevent or hinder the very process of change itself.

The keys to any successful quality initiative are now recognized as being found in the following points:

- strong customer focus;
- continuous improvement of processes;
- total involvement by all.

Perhaps the essential factor here is the continuous improvement of processes, for which traditional TQM uses seven principal tools:

1 histograms (frequency distributions);
2 cause-and-effect diagrams;
3 check sheets;
4 Pareto charts;
5 graphics;
6 control charts;
7 scatter diagrams.

Such tools are either aids to identifying root causes for process failures, or control tools to ensure process control. There are many other tools which have been added to this list during the 1980s and 1990s, mostly concerned with the development of new process as much as with existing process improvement.

A quality initiative adopted by a company must address issues to overcome resistance to change, and it has been found that the following are fundamental enablers for the TQM change process:

- a common vision for quality;
- management commitment and visible lead;
- corporate-wide education, training and support;
- adept problem-solving and ongoing process control.

As well as the successes, there have been a good number of failures, and in the long term TQM is perhaps falling from favour. More companies are relying heavily upon popular standardization approaches such as ISO 9000, and fewer on the more onerous but rewarding task of continuous process improvement. One reason for this is that TQM is too empirical in its application, and lacks both scientific foundation and a firm measure of success. Without a definite goal in view, and the embodied means by which progress and improvement can be measured, success with TQM cannot easily be judged. It is extremely difficult to motivate and justify what seems to be a repeated circular path, where in fact what is required is a spiralling (helix) process that moves forward at each revolution. ISO 9000, believed by many to be a step backwards from tried and tested TQM implementations, does at the very least have a final goal. Once a certificate has been achieved, quality standardization perhaps has little to motivate further improvement.

It must be stressed that part of the vision of Six Sigma is to serve as an 'agent of change'. The application is as much about changing organizations and attitudes as it is about statistics and metrics. Six Sigma would be a hollow vision indeed without the practical tools that a typical TQM approach can furnish. However, in return Six Sigma provides the much-needed vision, goal and metric, as well as bringing powerful analysis tools derived from Statistical Process Control together with a deeper understanding and appreciation of the normal distribution. Training and staff development are vital in any quality initiative. How much easier it is to explain facts and reality such as variation and normal distributions than it is to simply exhort people to deliver better customer service.

SIX SIGMA IN SERVICE INDUSTRIES

Ultimately, it is the partnership between all the aspects that comprise Six Sigma in its entirety that will ensure a long-lasting place for this methodology within future quality initiatives. The greatest challenge for Six Sigma in practice is to be found in non-manufacturing environments. If the methodology relies so heavily upon statistics, how can it be applied to an area where, traditionally, such measurements and analysis have often never set foot?

The reality is that *any* task is, in fact, a process, and exhibits variation similar to the normal distribution, and it *can* be measured and improved. The difficulty lies in bridging the gap between subjective issues such as what actually constitutes a defect, and concrete, measurable and actionable variables. However, this difficulty can be overcome.

Service industry is even more in need of Six Sigma quality initiatives than manufacturing, simply because output tends to go directly to customers, whereas in manufacturing most defects are either scrapped or fixed before shipping, and all a customer sees is the final batch. Service processes are also more complex and less robust than in manufacturing, and often there is virtually no history of design and control of anything except financial matters.

The reality is quite blunt. Consider again a supermarket checkout, where a customer approaches with 100 items in the Christmas shopping basket. For this customer, success in terms of the checkout process demands that it is fast and accurate. For such a process, manufacturing would have tolerances, scrap and rework procedures, and monitoring and control. To give supermarkets their due, checkout processes have improved dramatically in the major grocery chains during the 1990s, but there still exist major stores in the UK where it is simply not possible to price up 100 items without some problem or another. Failure to scan, retrieve a price look-up or enter a price accurately will immediately demonstrate that the process has no tolerance for failure: it stops, and rework is very expensive. As far as the customer is concerned – who is very much a part of the process – one defect actually means that the entire process is defective and a failure. No one walks away from a supermarket saying, 'That was 98 per cent successful,' but rather, 'They just can't get those cash registers to work.'

It is this ever-growing intolerance among human beings for experiencing failure that drives service industries into repeated quality initiatives. Every year, a new flavour of management consultancy suggests a variation on a theme of staff training, reward, encouragement or whatever.

No quality initiative in manufacturing would last for two minutes if it was suggested that talk or exhortation would make better cars. Measurement, analysis, consideration, improvement and then verification of the improvements are fundamental to any quality initiative today, and service industry cannot be different. Six Sigma has the tools and the power to cut ice where hot air has contributed little in the past.

SUMMARY

- Six Sigma stands for many things, including a metric, a philosophy, a goal, and a methodology.
- The philosophy of Six Sigma is *total customer satisfaction.*
- The goal of Six Sigma is to ensure almost zero customer defects in core customer processes.
- The statistical basis of Six Sigma is that:
  - all tasks are processes, and all processes exhibit variation;
  - most variation follows the normal distribution, which can be measured and understood;
  - the metric of Six Sigma is the distance between the mean of the outcome and the customer limits, measured in standard deviations or process sigma, and the new practical limit for perfection is obtained at six standard deviations either side of the mean;
  - the process sigma metric is often quoted in terms of defects, and an allowance of 1.5 sigma has been built into the calculations to account for long-term shift and spread.
- Six Sigma methodology relates to the practical application of the statistical theory, and can be applied equally well in both manufacturing and service industries. It brings together a number of existing tools and skills, such as Statistical Process Control and Total Quality Management, to aid with practical implementation.
- For manufacturing, the leap to low-cost quality has only taken place in conjunction with a transition from post-production product assurance to design and in-production customer-related quality.
- Service industries are inherently more complex and less tolerant of failure than manufacturing, and Six Sigma can provide the tools and insight needed to improve quality in this perhaps traditionally unfruitful area.

CHAPTER THREE

Understanding an Organization

Before any organization launches a Six Sigma quality initiative, it is vital that it understands itself fully. Six Sigma is such an all-encompassing change effort and requires so much management input and change within an organization that it cannot easily be applied to just part of a business or to a single process. It is also important to note that most organizations today are constructed around a group of functions, which do not necessarily align with customer-perceived processes. Change in the whole infrastructure of an organization is often one end-goal strategy for applying Six Sigma quality.

Every organization produces and delivers a mixture of products and services to its customers. To remain fit and competitive in the marketplace, businesses must deliver both quality and cost-effective products and services, which each add value for the customer. It is this added value which is the ultimate *raison d'être* for any business. Without added value, there will be few customers, and lack of customers is a certain recipe for failure.

Traditionally, consideration of product or service added value has been restricted to the entire organization. This is often seen in modern-day mission statements, which are almost always internally generated. It is far better to divide the organization into its constituent parts and to understand what exactly are the core products or services, and the processes by which they are delivered to the customer. A mission statement that declares 'we add value and quality to our products' is of little help. Far better to be open and honest and say that one particular product or process adds value, and the rest do not. Successful implementation of quality improvement must begin by laying the patient open to close and honest examination.

ADDING VALUE TO PRODUCTS AND SERVICES

Determining added value can be difficult, and is perhaps another area in which Six Sigma quality has yet to address a weakness. Figure 3.1 shows an approach to at least qualifying how added value affects services and products, and attempts to establish a more formal definition of 'luxury' than was considered in Chapter 1.

Consumers are human, and humans think in terms of straight lines. The 'consumer value perception line' shows that for consumers, a doubling in value has an associated doubling in costs; they are therefore prepared to pay for added value somewhere along or below this line. There are two important points, unique to each consumer, which define exactly where this line falls. The 'zero-cost value deficiency point' is what a consumer lacks by spending nothing. If this diagram were to represent the added value for, say, a washing machine, then this point is the lack of added value experienced by *not* buying a washing machine. It is this difference in added value that effectively drives the initial purchase. The 'minimal-cost point' is the consumer-perceived spend to obtain the minimal product, which by itself adds no more value than is absolutely necessary. The zero point on the 'added value' scale is 'obtain just what is needed'. This may be a basic washing machine that washes clothes but does no more, or indeed a trip to the launderette. The rest of the line now defines how much a consumer expects to pay in relation to an increase or decrease in added value.

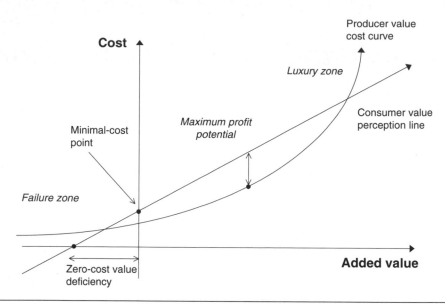

Figure 3.1 Added-value trade-off diagram

Against this line can be placed a curve representing the 'producer value cost', which goes some way towards indicating the real costs associated with adding value to a product or service. Improving on a basic washing machine costs very little, but by the time the machine has become 'state of the art', the costs climb rapidly for little return. Eventually, this curve passes through the consumer line, and it is at this point that luxury is reached. What a producer must charge for a product must be above this curve, and what the consumer is happy to pay must be on or below the 'consumer value perception line'. When the two lines pass, the consumer must pay over and above the perceived value. Luxury is indeed an advanced washing machine that sorts the clothes, washes, dries and then irons them.

There are four basic areas on this diagram, and only one of them describes a particularly good place for producers to be. The 'luxury zone' is reliant upon over-spend, in itself a fragile and insecure situation. The 'failure zone', often the result of poor quality, is where consumers perceive that they have less than the minimal cost option – or worse still, less than the zero-cost value point. For example, this is where a washing machine fails to do its job properly, and delivers less than the minimum expected, or floods the kitchen floor, leaving the consumer worse off than if they had not purchased it in the first place.

The point at which the producer cost curve cuts the 'cost' axis represents the production costs to deliver a zero added-value product or service. If this falls below the consumer perception of minimum cost, then it is possible to produce basic items at this point for a profit. However, if the curve is above the consumer minimum cost, then the producer cannot operate in this area, and fierce competition may drive low-value products off the market. Very few businesses can afford to sell a single nail or screw; profitability is generally only achieved when such items are sold in pre-packaged quantities.

The middle of the diagram shows the maximum profit area, where the vertical distance between producer cost and consumer value perception is at its greatest. A washing machine positioned here has plenty of added value, such as many wash options, an economy program, low

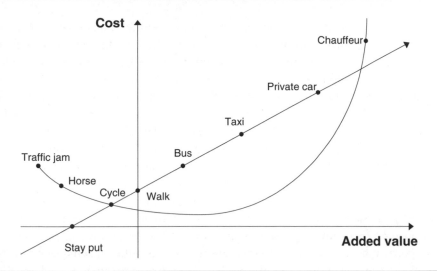

Figure 3.2   Example of added value for a simple service

water consumption, an interlocking door, an anti-flooding device and a casing painted a nice shade of green. None of this costs very much more than the basic machine, but the customer perception of the added value pays handsomely.

This diagram is somewhat qualitative and generalist, but it can grant an insight into the consumer's point of view and assist with long-term market placement strategy. Some of the UK supermarket chains are currently attempting to hedge their bets and position themselves at more than one point on this diagram. Tesco, for example, have a range of 'value' products that provide nothing more than the basic food item. Even the packaging is minimalist, and the product will sit at the zero added value point. The bulk of the market sits at the middle of the diagram, but the recent introduction of Tesco's 'finest' range is targeted towards the upper end of the diagram, bordering on luxury. There is a constant tendency for the entire marketplace to slowly but surely slide down the curve, as what was luxury becomes commonplace, and commonplace becomes of zero added value. It is, of course, in the producer's interest to always have new products arriving at the luxury end to fuel future markets. Constant careful positioning is necessary in order to reap the best possible return from the market, and maintaining products at the lower end as well as luxury items at the upper end ensures that all tastes are catered for.

Figure 3.2 shows the added-value trade-off diagram applied to a simple service situation, that of transport from A to B. The horse has been placed at a lower added value and higher cost, as the consumer perceives this particular 'solution' to be more onerous and less cost-effective. Being stuck in a traffic jam is perhaps worse than staying put, and could cost more overall. Such a diagram also reinforces the fact that consumer trends are always moving to higher added value, regardless of the costs involved.

It is never a particularly good idea to attempt to manipulate customer perceptions and expectations. However, if the slope of the consumer value perception line can be increased, more luxury items are brought into the standard marketing area and there is a general increase in profitability. Such a change can take place either by decreasing the zero-cost value deficiency, or by increasing the minimal-cost point. The converse is also very true, in that lowering the minimal-cost point lowers the line and changes the whole market.

It must also be stressed that this diagram describes nothing about quality. This may seem strange for a book principally about the subject of quality, but the point to note is that consumers purchase goods and services based on a trade-off between the costs and the added value obtained. Appropriate quality is expected at all levels of cost, and should have little or nothing to do with added value *per se*. Quality is satisfaction experienced as a result of a particular purchase, nothing more and nothing less. There is an increasing tendency on the part of producers and retailers to sell reliability rather than durability as part of the added value, which leads to poor consumer perception of the product, and a distortion of the diagram. Customer A purchases a basic washing machine for £200, and customer B purchases an advanced machine for £400. They both expect their machines to last (be durable) for about seven years, as washing machines in the UK usually do. Customer A has decided that a repeat spend of £200 every seven years is a good return for having a washing machine and not having to go to the launderette each week. Customer B, on the other hand, has decided that the additional features of the more expensive machine are worth the additional £200 every seven years. If either machine fails to return the appropriate added value over this period, this is evidence of poor quality, and reliability is an important factor in such quality perception. If the consumer is forced to pay an additional sum for reliability, either by buying breakdown warranty insurance or by not doing so and then running the risk of the implied repair bills, then reliability-quality has now been made part of the added value. This either forces consumers towards the lower-cost end (where the cost of the associated loss of added value is less) or heightens the frustration of gambling with a higher cost for what is probably less added value than at first appears. What can be included legitimately in the added-value equation is *durability*, which is associated with the intrinsic life and constitution of component parts. Customer C may wish to pay £500 for a washing machine, for which the parts are of a higher grade or specification (and therefore more durable, lasting perhaps ten years), in order to purchase additional life, and hence gain added value from reduced frequency of replacement or maintenance.

Confusion in this area can be considerable, and there is a natural tendency to speak of 'better-quality' components or manufacture, using the word 'quality' in a context where it appears to apply to cost and value, and can therefore be charged for. The considerable success of Far East products is due in part to excellent quality irrespective of cost, and such a way of thinking can only be achieved by firmly removing quality from the cost and added-value equation. One definition of 'value' – a term often used to justify prices – is 'fair equivalence'. It is true to say that the greater the slope of this line, the less customers will feel they are getting 'fair equivalence in value'. To be seen to offer good value therefore implies that the gradient of this line must be as shallow as possible, and this further implies that the producer cost curve must also be as low and flat as possible.

A STRATEGY FOR PRODUCTS AND SERVICES

Six Sigma is a methodology for improving and designing new processes. However, it does not have anything to say about any business in particular, and each individual organization has responsibility for ensuring that sense and reason exist in its long-term plans. Embarking on a Six Sigma quality initiative, whose first stage could run for at least three years, if not longer, provides an excellent opportunity to review and revise corporate strategy plans. Products, services or general business practices that are inappropriate, inefficient or ineffective should be put under a microscope and phased out if no long-term future is seen for them. Serious input is required for Six Sigma, and both short- and long-term results must be expected in return; there is little point in wasting such effort on dead-end products or services with no market future.

Several major players world-wide today are using Six Sigma to revolutionize their company performance, and each has a well-structured and well-implemented strategy into which such a quality initiative has been carefully introduced. Six Sigma is important, but it is not the be-all and end-all, and such companies position Six Sigma as part of their strategy for globalization, better market share and improved shareholder value. For some organizations, Six Sigma quality has only been introduced after several preparatory initiatives have been launched year on year, each such initiative building on the previous and adding value to the global strategy plan, and each also ultimately paving the way for Six Sigma itself.

The overall success of any company depends upon many factors, and quality is only one. To ensure outstanding success, every organization must consider how best to position itself in the market, to drive results and make use of the resources and assets available. Through understanding the products and services offered, and the market environment in which they are placed, aware-ness will emerge of how quality can best be used as a key differentiator. After everything has been analysed and considered, it must be every organization's wish that customers beat a path to its door and demand to buy what is on offer, and then for the organization to be able to meet such demand. Outstanding quality in products and services has the potential to support more focused drives to:

● penetrate newer and wider markets;
● consolidate a better existing market share;
● retain a greater proportion of customers at renewal.

Whatever market an organization chooses to operate within, being the fastest, best-value, most reliable and, above all, most consistent will ultimately ensure customer loyalty and increase profit-ability.

At an early stage, a strategic evaluation of the current state of the organization is essential, and should attempt to answer at least the following points:

● What is the present overall competitive position?
● Does the company have an appropriate mission statement?
● What are the company's objectives, in both the short term and the long term?
● What are the key strategies the organization will use to achieve its objectives?
● How do external customers view the organization?
● How do internal staff view the organization?
● To what extent does successful teamwork operate within the company?
● How are 'quality' and 'change' seen generally, and what role does quality currently play?

One of the most revealing assessments that can be carried out is to detail to what extent a sense of a need for change exists within a business. As organizations grow and develop in size and struc-ture, pockets of inefficient and inappropriate processes emerge and begin to spread. Caused as much by a 'big company' attitude, management structures and fiscal controls can also raise barriers to natural and continuous process improvement. The many employees at the sharp end of any business process are often acutely aware of a need for change, but are either unwilling or unable to carry out improvements. Cultural desire for change must commence at the very top of an organization, and without open and honest management little will be achieved, even with the best will in the world. It required a visitation from three spirits, of Christmas past, present and future, to convince Scrooge that a change was needed for his own good. Likewise, many organizations need to consider what has been, what is now, and what is to be if nothing radical changes, in order to kindle the spark of the need for change.

CORE AND ENABLING PROCESSES

A look around any organization today will reveal a string of departments called by such names as Marketing, Sales, Customer Services, Finance, Information Technology, Human Resources, Shipping, Production, Design and Development, and so on. It is useful to start by defining the core products and services that an organization produces and delivers, and then list all the internal functions that go to make up the entire business. Key and revealing questions that can be asked at this point are:

- How well do products and services relate to individual functions?
- What is the added value delivered for each product or service?
- Which department adds greatest value, and which the least?
- How many departments touch the customer directly or affect customer quality?
- What inherent waste and inefficiency exists in these functions?

Organizations that have commenced or already adopted ISO 9000 or similar will have begun to answer a great many questions about internal structure, and in a number of cases businesses will have used process mapping to describe much of the operational heart of the organization. Process mapping is an excellent tool to use, both to describe processes (pictures are worth a thousand words) and to reveal the extent of waste and inappropriate work that is currently being carried out. Benchmarking is a valuable tool within Six Sigma, and an organization is well advised to describe and measure itself fully before beginning any work on improvements.

Figure 3.3 sets out the principal elements in any detailed process map. The high-level SIPOC map was introduced in Chapter 2, when considering the fact that everything is a process. The

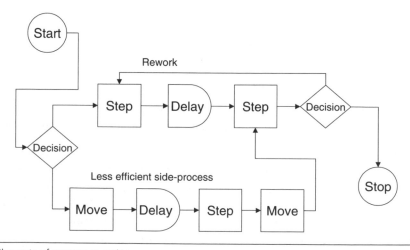

Figure 3.3 Elements of process mapping

SIPOC map is further expanded by detailed process mapping to a level that demonstrates areas of inefficiency and waste. Process maps commence and finish at start and stop points, and pass through a series of individual process steps with decision points and inefficient delays or moves.

Such elemental process steps can be further divided into sub-processes and even micro-processes, as required. The essential aim of process mapping is to provide an accurate description of reality, but only to such a level as can be beneficial for process improvement; excessive detail will often hide the wood among the trees.

Process mapping allows a full consideration of what are *core* and *enabling* processes, and the identification of added-value, enabling and non-added-value process steps. Customers are only interested in processes and process steps that add value, and anything else, for them at least, adds no benefit. The formal definition of 'added value' can be very restrictive, and is often cited as something for which customers will pay, either fiscally or in time or effort. Using this definition to identify processes that matter to customers will show that very little does indeed matter. At the process step level, individual processes either add value, or enable an organization to execute the process, or add no intrinsic value to either side. Processes are most likely to have at their heart a physical entity, which is transformed by adding value during the process, and looking for a physical change to the entity is the easiest way to identify added-value steps, for which customers will also gladly pay. Further, such steps must be carried out the first time, as repeating any step for whatever reason does not add any further value – indeed, often quite the reverse.

It is probably as well to consider an example at this point, and return to the supermarket checkout queue. In manufacturing, it is much easier to identify physical entities at the heart of processes, such as refrigerators and motor cars. For a service-dominated industry such as retailing, only the purchased goods are physical entities, and in some cases, such as legal advice or consultancy, there may be no visible physical entity at all. For a supermarket, the added value for customers lies in being able to identify, gather and collect, and then transport home items they require. Here, the supermarket is fulfilling a basic need for grocery produce, and adding value by making the process of obtaining such items easier. The alternative (often a good way of identifying added value) may be for the customer to visit many more shops, or spend more money and time, or perhaps even find alternative sources. For the customer, the only processes and process steps that add value are those which move the ultimate goal closer, and for a supermarket (as in retailing in general), this principally involves identifying, finding, gathering and shipping goods. This covers such things as producing a shopping list, going to the store, walking round and taking items off the shelf, and then loading the car.

For the supermarket, there are many other processes, such as purchasing and delivering to stores the goods to be sold, keeping goods in marketable condition, advertising and pricing – and, of course, being paid. All of these, together with finance and accounting, information technology, customer services and so on, enable the supermarket to perform the value-adding tasks. Without information technology, most organizations today would not exist, but very few IT departments actually add value directly for customers. Buried in all of this will be a number of processes and process steps that have no value, either direct or indirect. These are such steps as moves and delays or rework. Moving goods from a wholesaler to a supermarket is a borderline case, as it really adds no value for the customer – the goods could go directly to the customer's home – however, it does enable the supermarket to display and allow customers to identify and purchase goods. Moving goods around the store is also questionable, and can only enable or add value if it assists customers to find and collect purchases. Certainly, pricing items individually has traditionally added no value for the customer, and simply enabled the retailer to conduct the payment step correctly. Any errors in pricing which require re-pricing simply add rework to what has already gone before, which is a perfect example of waste and inefficiency. The delay between stocking a shelf and a customer taking the item is also wasted time and effort, and costs the retailer real time and money in providing stock and storage facilities.

It is the eventual aim of any sound TQM initiative to enhance the value-adding steps, to make the enabling steps more efficient, and to remove the non-value-adding steps. So, what of the checkout queuing process? Certainly, this is an enabling process, as it enables the supermarket to charge each customer for their purchases correctly, and without it retailers would not operate. It does not add value for the customer, except perhaps by providing a receipt, or physically changing the entity which is 'customer account' to 'paid'. Looking at the process in detail, we find:

1 waiting in a queue (delay, wasted time);
2 unloading all the goods (enabling for pricing, but wasted customer effort);
3 scanning (enabling, and adding some value, since it changes the 'customer account');
4 reloading the purchases into bags (wasted rework);
5 payment (added value, since it changes the 'customer account').

Ideally, for the customer this process would be simply a payment which credits their 'account' and allows them to depart. For the supermarket, this process would be an accurate log of what is purchased and paid for, enabling other processes such as restocking to be carried out more effectively. With this in mind, some supermarkets have improved this process so that it does only include the value-adding and enabling steps. Consumers can scan their own purchases, and load them directly into boxes to take home. Queuing is reduced or eliminated, there is no unloading and reloading, and there is an improved payment process. The essence of TQM is to continue such improvement to its logical conclusion, so that each organization constitutes only value-added or enabling processes and process steps wherein the maximum is gained from the value-adding steps, and the minimum is expended on the enabling steps.

Examples of core processes

As a general guideline for businesses, it is possible to arrive at a simplified set of typical core processes and underlying enabling functions. Unifying this for both manufacturing and service industries is quite difficult, and Figure 3.4 is a conglomeration of several more specific examples. In itself, it is unlikely to fit any single organization particularly well, and will need to be modified and adjusted to suit. However, the basic principles remain that a few elemental processes are core to the organizational structure and to the value added for the customer.

There are really only five core steps for any product or service for which customers are prepared to pay. The expectation of customers is that organizations will:

1 conceive of a (new) product or service to meet a customer need;
2 market the product or service to match solution to need;
3 deliver the product or service;
4 support the product or service beyond initial purchase;
5 attempt to retain ongoing customer loyalty.

These five high-level process steps can each be further divided into two or three sub-steps that move closer to the real-life operation of each organization. Behind the core processes are the

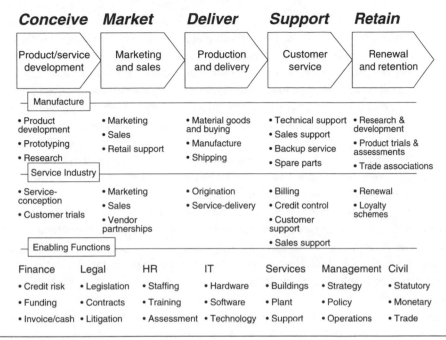

Figure 3.4 Typical core processes

enabling functions, which customers in general take for granted and strictly do not view as adding value. The further benefit of considering core processes separately from enabling functions is that core processes generally align well with customer perceptions about how an organization delivers products and services. Placing greater emphasis on such core processes than lesser enabling functions gives the customer viewpoint predominance, which is exactly what Six Sigma purports to do. Let us consider two examples, one from manufacturing, and the other very much service-related.

Refrigerator-manufacturing core processes

The fundamental customer need that is resolved by purchasing a refrigerator is that of keeping food fresh. Any consumer of produce such as milk will appreciate the need to prevent excessive temperatures from promoting mould and bacterial growth and the destruction of such comestibles. By rushing out to purchase a suitable device (which in itself is a service industry solution to a need), consumers are acknowledging that the manufacturer of such a product has added value to a heap of raw materials. The final product adds more than just shaping and forming materials into a refrigerator, in that it has also been designed to be suitable for a particular solution to a particular set of needs. More than one need may be solved by any one refrigerator. For example, aesthetics and size are important considerations in the typical home. An American-style unit would generally be excessively large and perhaps unsuited to British cultural expectations of a 'fridge'.

Consumers are very willing to pay for the step that conceives such solutions, and the next step that markets and makes products available. If this were not the case, consumers would just purchase metal boxes that kept things cold. What actually happens is that consumers pay to have more novel and up-to-date solutions, such as fridge-freezers, built-in models and modern colour schemes. Consumers also want to be able to locate such products easily, and expect companies to promote and advertise their wares. Nothing is more infuriating than not being able to locate the ideal solution, and together, these steps are ones that some consumers will even pay to have completed by a third party. Kitchen designers and installers, as well as house-builders, will often bundle refrigerators and the like into one complete package.

The step that is central to the consumer solution is the actual production of such manufactured items. Here, raw materials are shaped and worked into a consummate whole whose performance is greater than the sum of the individual parts. The majority of the consumer market is highly indifferent to the technical issues and manufacturing process, and simply perceives the product as a white or black box performing a given task. As long as it does the job, there is little interest in the exact processes by which the refrigerator is constructed, and it must be this construction step, if any, which attracts the greatest added value. Certainly, it is the only step that is entirely indispensable, even to the most self-sufficient and robust customer.

It is the point of 'doing the job' – solving the need – which leads to a slight departure from pure manufacturing and leads into the area of customer service. No manufacturing organization today is allowed, even if it is unwilling, to simply sell a product to a customer and then depart without providing ongoing support and backup services. The customer expectation, for which real payment is often made in terms of warranty insurance, is that help will be there when help is needed. Modern manufacturing has extended this ideal to providing websites to market and support products, and many consumer goods are involved in extensive repair and after-sales support networks. The market for motor car consumables is extensive, and a small industry exists to manufacture and supply spare parts, as well as to provide technical support and advice.

By their very nature, people are resistant to change and have a very high level of brand loyalty, particularly in regard to the more expensive consumer products. The modern consumer, faced with ever-larger global organizations, can solve a range of needs by patronizing one company, and considerable personal pride and comfort can be gained by doing so. For example, the Philips organization has a reputation for development of products that exhibit technical lead and excellence, even if not necessarily market leadership. As well as refrigeration, this company, like many others, can offer a wide range of white goods and domestic electrical items. Once a purchase has proven to be satisfying on all counts, typical consumer reaction is to remain with a trusted partner, and again consumers are willing to pay for this. They do, however, expect something in return, and being let down by a bad product from a well-known brand name is very disappointing.

Close examination of Figure 3.4 will show that the last process step – retain – has similarities to the first step, and may have sub-processes which can equally well fit into either position. Just as quality is a continuous process of improvement, manufacture is also a continuous spiral in which the producer aims always to improve the solution that meets the customer's needs.

Products from manufacturing cover a vast range in terms of complexity, cost, market position and consumer need. Not every item will fit such an idealistic core process pattern, and it may well be that the less complex end of the spectrum can ignore all except the middle core process. This may well be the reason why many manufacturing companies still remain at a distance from the real end consumer.

Teashop service core processes

Service-related industry in general has traditionally prided itself on a high level of customer service, yet it remains almost entirely aloof from in-depth inspection and analysis. Ultimately, there cannot be a vast difference between service and manufacturing, and it is to be expected that the high-level core processes will be very similar. Even in service industry, a product can usually be identified, albeit intangible in some cases. For example, let us consider a simple teashop, and in this case the product is a serving of tea or coffee, for which popular consumer demand is as high as ever. There can be little doubt that in such markets, the service offered is more important than the product delivered. Reflection upon the past ten restaurants visited when dining out is more likely to lead to recollection of poor service than details of the menu or exactly what was eaten. Popping in for a cup of tea is as much about pausing to sit and chat as it is about drinking something, and the pleasurable experience from good service and nice surroundings (or not, as the case may be) will often surpass that of the drink itself. The consumers' needs are much more complex in services than in manufacturing, and undoubtedly more short-term and fickle. There are examples of service industries where the cup of tea is all that customers are seeking, such as fast-food and take-away outlets, but this is similar to the lower end of the manufacturing industry spectrum, where not all the core processes under consideration may be evident.

The first core process is again one of conception. The creation and development of services are probably more evident to customers than they are in the case of products, and for a teashop this includes such things as the menu, service arrangements and the environment for the service-delivery, as well as the type of tea used. Novelty and entertainment are both strongly associated with services, as the needs of customers now extend beyond simple products to more ethereal concepts. Considerable added value is attached to the space and the manner in which tea is served, and customers are happy to pay a premium for the process that delivers these points. The 'Palm Court' tea room, complete with live chamber music, can charge above the standard rate, even if only for a select customer market. The perfect setting for an excellent cup of tea requires much more than the product itself, as the Japanese tea ceremony demonstrates.

Marketing is also highly evident within service industries, again perhaps since the intangible service itself has to be touted along with the tangible product. Teashops of all varieties are well window-dressed to ensure that potential customers can locate such services easily and know exactly what to expect. A fridge is a fridge – at least underneath the glossy exterior that matches the kitchen units. The distinction between 'Joe's Café' and 'Palm Court' is considerable, even if both serve exactly the same brand of tea. Consumers are perhaps more intolerant of mismatch between needs and services than needs and products, and the expectation is that (unconsciously at least) service marketing will be accurate, extensive and maybe even flamboyant.

The main core process is again the provision of the service/product – being served with a cup of tea – and again the emphasis is very much on *how*, as well as on *what*. The follow-on customer service may not always be distinguishable as a separate process for such short-term instances as a teashop. Self-service establishments have reduced any customer service following the initial provision of fare to the act of clearing away afterwards, which in itself is perhaps more an enabling function than a core process. Only where there is an ongoing relationship between customer and provider does the support core process become evident. Such relationships between customer and service-provider are very fragile, and often service industry fails to consider what happens once the initial service is over. Small organizations, which are close to customers, may take feedback seriously and develop the business to retain loyal custom. Taking table reservations for local repeat customers at the 'Palm Court' is one way of extending the customer service through the retention core process to close the loop.

A more substantial example of service core processes can be seen in the consideration of modern supermarket chains. Here, the conception step is very prominent in the development of out-of-town large supermarkets, which have blossomed to provide the mainstay of UK grocery shopping over the past two decades. Over time, consumers expect more and more, and will move allegiance to stores which extend the concept by providing more than just a grocery shopping facility. Marketing is also an important process, as much about placing stores in the locality as it is about selling the brand image. Beyond the essential process of actually presenting and selling goods to consumers, customer service is now a major differentiator for the leading chains, and the introduction of loyalty cards (to replace the trading-stamps of old) has firmly placed the retention core process back on the agenda of retailing today. No one would now think of providing less than six different varieties of supermarket shopping trolley to meet the specific needs of shoppers. Consumers, who are likely to pay more for the service, welcome the provision of such amenities, and hence trolleys have moved from being part of an enabling process to being part of a core process.

All core processes should be identified and fully considered when implementing either new strategies or quality initiatives. Recent developments in Internet grocery shopping show clearly that a fundamental change in one core process has implications for the rest of the business, and it is folly to replace one part without carefully considering the rest. Developing an alternative to the central core process and removing the need to actually visit stores is a radical alteration to the fundamental business engaged in by supermarket retailers. This really amounts to introducing a completely new business, and as such, it needs new core processes for conception, marketing, customer service and retention. If supermarkets have come so far over the past decade by improving customer service, such customer service core processes must be seen in new business ventures conducted via the Internet.

Enabling functions

The man on the street corner who sells roasted chestnuts during winter is the epitome of efficiency, and probably needs almost no enabling functions. He has the concept and marketing core processes, and all the service- and product-delivery, together with excellent customer service. By being at the same place day to day and season to season, he will also engender retention and loyalty. Extending the business does not mean that customers will be willing to accept greater cost to pay for additional processes, such as storage, a separate cashing department, shipping and staff training. All these things the customer sees as being of no added value. Who needs a finance department to roast chestnuts? Only, perhaps, a large organization, where the size of operation dictates the need for such additional processes. Enabling functions tend to be most efficient when operating across a number of core processes – the core process is aligned to the flow expected by customers, and the enabling function is aligned to discrete business units. In this way, finance, for example, could provide facilities for many different sub-core processes. If transport is needed, then perhaps this is best provided by an enabling transport function, which can transport goods, staff, produce and even customers to maximum benefit and efficiency, rather than being spread out across many core processes. Such internal efficiency drives can cause conflict over resource allocation between processes, however, and are not always a good idea.

Whether a process is core and has added value or is an enabling one is often dependent on the expectations of particular customers. For example, fast-food outlets in the UK normally expect most customers to clear away their own waste, and very little clearing effort is required from staff. In the same brand outlet in Sweden, customers actually sort their waste for recycling into different bins, and in Austria almost no one expects to clear anything away at all, requiring extra staff to perform this task. The simple process of clearing a table is part of a high-level core process, an enabling process, or a non-value-adding process step depending entirely on (local) customer expectations. If there is any lesson to be learnt, it must be that nothing can be taken for granted, and that customers' perception of the value of a process is likely to shift over time.

Service and manufacturing overlap

It should be noted that there is considerable overlap between manufacturing and service industries. Figure 3.4 shows 'customer service' within manufacturing industry, and 'delivery of service/product' within service industry. No product can be brought to market without customer support, which in itself embodies all the aspects of pure service, and likewise very few service industries exist without a tangible product for which purely manufacturing aspects are ideally suited. In developing and introducing Six Sigma to their organization in the 1980s, Motorola did not initially apply the concept and methods outside the manufacturing sector of its business. In contrast, General Domestic Appliances, which introduced Six Sigma during 1998, immediately applied the quality initiative across all departments and functions, with positive benefits in all areas.

There is also often a blurring between where one manufacturing industry ends and another service industry commences. In setting out to purchase a refrigerator, consumers are interacting with a retail service industry which identifies products, markets them, conducts a sales process, provides post-sales support, and then attempts to retain customer loyalty. For the consumer, it is as if the retailer had manufactured the product, or perhaps as if the manufacturer had sold the product. Whichever, it is not in the interests of either retailer or manufacturer to remain aloof and in isolation from each other, as the customer's sole interest is a seamless solution to a need. Organizations have typically extended quality initiatives only to their own boundaries, controlling input and output standards to meet other organizations' respective output and input standards. Such isolationist tactics are reinforced by heavy-handed standardization, and this is something that is wholly inappropriate to a customer-driven quality initiative. World-class Six Sigma companies are moving towards joint initiatives with suppliers and principal customers, where a more united quality initiative hands over some responsibility and authority beyond the immediate boundaries of the business.

SUMMARY

- For a successful approach to Six Sigma, an organization needs to first understand and appraise its own worth and position in the marketplace. The principal reason for the existence of a business is to add value to a product or service, and this added value is related to cost, not quality.
- Each organization delivers a mix of products and services through a set of processes. Processes can be mapped down to individual steps, which are either value-adding, enabling or non-value-adding.
- The main core processes are those which constitute the essential operation, add value for the customer and map well onto customer perceptions of the delivery of the product and/or service. In general, they are:
  1 conceive;
  2 market;
  3 deliver;
  4 support;
  5 retain.

● The identification of specific core processes and enabling functions needs to be an ongoing task which each organization undertakes as an early part of any quality or change initiative.
● The aim of a quality initiative must be to enhance core processes, make the enabling functions more efficient, and remove all other waste and non-value-adding process steps.

CHAPTER FOUR

Understanding the Customer

Much has been written about customers in the earlier chapters, and it can be rightly said that it is the customer who is central to the philosophy of Six Sigma. Putting the customer first is not new by any means, but it has an entirely new significance within Six Sigma, where the aim is to completely satisfy – if not exceed – the customer's requirements.

Each organization decides for itself exactly what it will bring to the marketplace in terms of products and services, but thereafter everything must be done hand-in-hand with, and for, the anticipated customer. Organizations must be able to identify customers and their associated needs, and then drive change within the business to ensure that core processes run with the sole aim of delivering to customer expectations. The key to success in this is the ability to identify and turn customer needs into *measurable* and *actionable* characteristics against which the quality of a product or service can be gauged and improved.

To see exactly where this leads, consider the supermarket example in Chapter 3. Questioning departing customers may reveal that some are not satisfied with the checkout process, in that it is too slow and inaccurate. After analysis, this may consolidate to a customer need for a 'prompt and accurate checkout process'. From the core processes identified in Chapter 3, a complete tree of customer requirements can be constructed, and within this, the customers' needs can be listed, perhaps as in Figure 4.1.

This is quite an elaborate tree, showing part of the breakdown for just the one core process of 'shopping'. Each core process can be divided into sub-processes, and so on until firm and indivisible customer requirements are located. In addition, with care, it is possible to weight each level of the tree, and so arrive at an intrinsic importance for each requirement. In this particular example (which is fictitious), customers have indicated that the shopping process contributes 80 per cent towards overall satisfaction. Within this process, the sub-process of 'purchase' is 60 per cent of satisfaction, the rest of the sub-processes being 'identify goods', 'locate and collect' and 'transport'. Again, the purchase element has been divided into 'checkout' and 'telephone order', with the requirements for the checkout element amounting to 'promptness' and 'accuracy'.

Working backwards from this, it would be possible to say that for this supermarket to be seen as a quality organization, among other considerations the checkout process must be prompt. Specifically, just this one element of quality contributes 30 per cent of 90 per cent of 60 per cent of 80 per cent, or approximately 13 per cent. Working through all the customer requirements in a similar way builds a complete picture of what must be achieved to deliver excellent quality. Further, by careful analysis, specific values can be attributed to each requirement, turning them into Critical To Quality (CTQ) characteristics. To satisfy customers, promptness might be 'start checkout within two minutes of queuing' and 'take no more than 15 seconds per item', both of which must be completely met to satisfy the 'average customer'.

Readers will have noticed that in Chapter 3, checkout queuing was not seen as a core process, but an enabling one, and yet here it has been placed back into the core processes of shopping. This is a clear disjuncture, in that (for this example) the checkout process is not core to the delivery of the service/product, but it is important to customer satisfaction, and hence quality. This makes it even more important that the service-delivery is first-class, as failure to meet

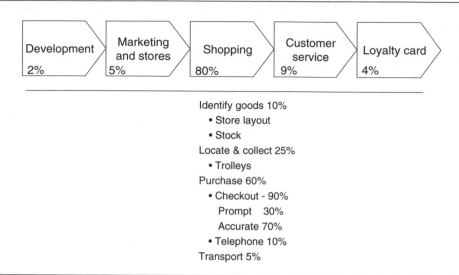

Figure 4.1 Part of a CTQ tree

customer requirements will certainly result in a loss of custom, and hence this element of service has been added back into the organization's core processes model. Core process maps are idealistic representations of that which adds value, whereas CTQ trees are realistic representations of precise customer requirements for experienced satisfaction and quality.

EXTERNAL CUSTOMERS

Any person not directly connected with an organization who touches the processes of the organization in any way is an external customer. The most obvious customers are those who consume products or services. However, suppliers, for example, can also be customers, as they touch the billing and payment processes at some point. It is the external customer who has predominant importance within the quality initiative.

Customers can be divided into three classes:

1 customers;
2 not-customers;
3 non-customers.

Active *customers* are those normally regarded as dealing, or having dealt with, an organization in some way during the previous day, week, month or year, depending on the product or service. For refrigerators, customers are likely to remain so for the life of the product, but supermarket customers may last only as long as it takes to walk away from the store. *Not-customers* are potential, existing or past customers who have gone elsewhere, and they are not customers (any more). They are of particular interest, as they were once customers and are no longer, or have made a distinct choice not to consume the product or service and have gone elsewhere. On the other hand, although the difference may seem small, *non-customers* are potential customers who have not consumed (or are not consuming now) a given product or service at all, or who are actively using an altogether different market segment. The person walking in through the supermarket door to buy milk is a customer, the person walking in through a competitor's supermarket door to buy milk is a not-customer, and the person who has milk delivered to the doorstep in the traditional British way is a non-customer. Each class is of particular interest in a quality initiative, as non-customers and not-customers may have more to say about poor quality and value-add than do existing customers. It is, of course, in the interests of any organization to increase its market share by reaching new customers and retaining existing customers through excellent quality.

INTERNAL CUSTOMERS

The output of one process often becomes the input of another process, especially in the context of the internal operations of an organization. In particular, some of the enabling functions of a business are often almost wholly internally related, such as finance and information technology. The internal customer is of equal importance to the running and smooth operation of an organization, although there is often no direct link to bottom-line profit. Internal customers are often also stakeholders, in that they have a close interest in the operation and success of the business. This is very much the case with the shareholder, who is principally interested in the intrinsic value and worth of the business, and return on investment. The employees of an organization are inherently involved with the day-to-day running and operational issues, and have a considerable stake in the overall outcome of any business. Other stakeholders may include regulatory bodies and creditors, each of which has an interest. Such internal customers often have little influence over strategy and operational control, but do have a considerable impact on business success. To be fully effective, any quality initiative must address every aspect that leads to customer satisfaction, and do so for each customer.

An easy way to divide and conquer the entire quality issue is to split it into three regions:

1 customers;
2 processes;
3 employees.

In the *customer* region, Six Sigma quality aims to provide total satisfaction and to meet customers' needs fully. This can, and indeed should, include such considerations as profitability and corporate safety for the shareholder. In *processes*, Six Sigma looks to improvement and defect-reduction, which provides not only external customer satisfaction, but also improvement in internal efficiency. In the area of *employees*, Six Sigma promotes the idea of a valued employee, who is trained, motivated and regarded as an asset. In this way, the quality initiative becomes a win–win–win situation. It is a win for the customer, who experiences excellent quality; it is a win for the company, which sees reduced costs and improved profits; and it is a win for the employee, who becomes more valued and more engaged within the operation of a successful business.

It should be noted that for service industries, the consumer is often the supplier as well as the customer. In telephoning a call centre to request information, for example, the caller is both supplier of the information required and the customer of the outcome, which might be a mailed letter. This dual role leads to a greater need and pressure for excellent quality, and makes the task doubly difficult for the company, as it is not so easy to pass customer requirements back down to the supplier. In the retail trade, it is often possible to simply hand customer requirements back down to suppliers, as many top high-street stores currently do, driving quality by berating suppliers to do better.

CUSTOMER SATISFACTION

A fundamental measure of quality is the satisfaction that a customer experiences with a process and its outcome. There can be no doubt that a satisfied customer is more likely to remain a customer, to repeat business, and to refer others to the organization. A dissatisfied customer, however, is likely not only to cease their custom, but also to tell others about poor experiences. Such behavioural patterns differ considerably from one market sector to another, but in general it is regarded that a satisfied customer is up to seven times more likely to repeat business, and that a dissatisfied customer will verbalize discontent to perhaps 16 other people.

It is quite possible to measure customer satisfaction on a percentage scale, and the basic tools and techniques used provide the means by which Six Sigma quality initiatives can also learn from customers. The principal steps are:

1 Identify customers and customer segments.
2 Clarify core processes, and their relevance to customers.
3 Gain insight into current business and quality weaknesses.
4 Identify customer needs, and convert these to requirements.
5 Transform requirements into actionable Critical To Quality characteristics.
6 Monitor ongoing performance.

Many organizations gather feedback from customers by means of surveys, focus groups, point-of-sale information and complaints, and so on. Six Sigma requires both general customer information and feedback to paint an overview picture, and also highly specific information that will eventually lead to firm CTQs, which in turn drive the quality improvement and measurement of success. Points 2, 4 and 5 in the above list are more specific to Six Sigma than to a more general Total Quality Management strategy, and these important issues will be covered in more depth later in this chapter. The key to success is to listen carefully to the customer and hear what they are saying. The raw, verbatim information is often called the 'voice of the customer', and one of the more difficult stages in a Six Sigma quality programme involves gathering a sufficient quantity of customer information of sufficient quality, and then converting such material into sensible and useful conclusions.

Identifying customers and customer segments

Before surveying customers, it is important to understand the customer base fully, and segment out the different groups that may exist. Typically, customer research is directed at the Decision Making Unit (DMU) which has the influence when purchasing goods and services. Knowing the composition and make-up of the DMU will assist in both basic surveying and identifying defect opportunities later on. The 'buying' process typically involves:

● recognizing a need;
● determining a specification for a solution;
● searching for information;
● evaluating alternatives;
● making decisions;
● outcomes.

In the simple case of basic consumers, the DMU is normally one person, and the buying process is much simplified. However, most organizations will have a range of customers in terms of geographical location, demographics, DMU complexity and level of sophistication. It may take several months of specialist research to identify the essential differentiating factors within the customer base before any further and more detailed work can progress. It must also be stressed that non-customers and not-customers should be identified and included in any research. Exploratory research can usually identify basic issues with regard to quality at the same time as sketching out the various customer segments; immediate use can often be made of such early information, making the time, effort and costs involved seem less of a burden.

Clarifying core processes

It will almost invariably be the case that the factors that matter to an organization are not quite the same as those that matter to the customer. It is this disjuncture between organization and customer that gives rise to many of the quality issues in the first place, and it could be very tempting to rush into Six Sigma by defining core processes and customer requirements solely from the business point of view. Chapter 3 outlined the need to define core processes, and most of this work is completed from internal analysis of the business structure. Now comes the time to go to the customer base and clarify such core processes in the cold light of day. The business definition of 'core' will be 'that which adds value to the customer', whereas the customer definition of 'core' will be 'that which matters (adds value) and affects satisfaction and perceived quality'. In most cases, the shift in perspective will not give rise to any great change. However, as discussed above, some processes can affect customer satisfaction even when they add no intrinsic value. The only reliable way to identify core and enabling processes is to ask the customer, and the trap to studiously avoid is making assumptions on their behalf. An additional benefit of customer-clarification will be the quantifiable ranking of such processes against customer judgement. During the later stages in Six Sigma, it is of outstanding benefit to be able to point to any particular process and confidently assign a numerical value for the customer-held importance of that process.

Gaining business insight

The main reason why any organization conducts any form of customer research at all is to find out how satisfied the customer is, and what they think about the business and its products and services, both current and future. Where such research is conducted outside a Six Sigma initiative, the aims will generally be to quantify customer satisfaction, perhaps look for areas of concern, or to make a more informed choice between possible alternatives in product or service features. There is no reason why customer research specifically undertaken as part of a Six Sigma initiative should be treated any differently. When customer information begins to emerge from research, it can be put to good use generally, and feedback and action applied to existing areas of concern. Some of the information that will emerge from customer research may not necessarily be directly applicable or useful to the Six Sigma initiative in the short term, since the principal aim of Six Sigma customer research is ultimately to arrive at specific CTQ characteristics for each process. Findings such as the fact that the average customer does not know who you are, or thinks that your product is made by a competitor, really apply only to high-level business strategy and future direction. Making good use of all the information returned, both from a traditional customer-research aspect as well as a Six Sigma approach, will increase the return on the investment made, and ensure that customer analysis is an ongoing and well-used business tool.

Identifying customer needs and requirements

Excellent quality is associated with satisfied customers, and customer satisfaction comes from fully meeting deep-seated customer needs and requirements. It is therefore vital to capture the essential characteristics of products, services and processes that directly or indirectly give rise to customer satisfaction, and to list these as well-defined customer needs and requirements for each process. This step can be difficult to carry out, since often even the customers themselves are not consciously aware of their own needs and requirements, and it is important to explore fully all aspects of a process to locate every conceivable element that affects customer satisfaction. Any person walking into a supermarket has requirements for, and expectations of, the checkout process, such as the time taken, how much queuing is involved, and the accuracy of the billing processes. Major problems with service-related quality often arise because one or more of these customer needs have been overlooked or taken for granted. Safety and accuracy, for example, are always vital to good service and are critically important to almost every customer of any process, and failure to deliver as expected dramatically curtails customer satisfaction, and hence quality. In contrast, more and more organizations are realizing that customer market share can be won rapidly, easily and effectively by surpassing customer expectation, and by providing solutions to needs customers were not aware of or had no expectation of being met by the process.

From requirements to Critical To Quality characteristics

Customer needs and requirements, such as 'lack of queuing' and 'checkout speed', in themselves do not generally align well with real, day-to-day process issues that are both measurable and open to change and improvement. One of the arduous aspects of the Six Sigma approach is the appropriate translation of often fuzzy and intangible customer 'wants' to firm and measurable Critical To Quality characteristics with defined numerical limits and targets. Only when an organization has arrived at a set of well-defined CTQs can the process of quality measurement and improvement begin in earnest. Scientific and repeatable measurement is the basis for the Six Sigma approach, and it is necessary to determine a list of CTQ characteristics for processes that are not only measurable, but also actionable. Such customer needs as 'speed' and 'no queuing' must be converted into CTQs such as 'takes no more than one minute to reach a cashier' and 'checkout process takes no longer than ten seconds per item'. The success of the Six Sigma approach to customer quality depends entirely upon the ability to link such CTQs forward to potential process improvement and back to customer satisfaction. Only when this is achieved is it possible to action process change that can be both measured and guaranteed to have an impact on quality. The one CTQ for checkout speed (there may be several CTQs for each process) which states that 'each item is processed within ten seconds' is clearly measurable, and it will be possible to determine how often this target is not attained, and also perhaps why. It will also be possible to change the process and measure improvement, but perhaps more importantly, the extensive customer research conducted will have shown clearly that this relates firmly to the need for speed, and thus directly affects satisfaction with the process and overall customer-perceived quality.

Ongoing monitoring

It can be far too easy to take a quick 'snapshot' of the state of an organization, act on the results, and then return to a position of relative complacency and lethargy, only to be woken with a jolt the next time customer information is urgently required. Only organizations that regard customer research as a valuable, continuous business tool will persist in seeing benefit from the information and insight gleaned. As the process of customer research is often expensive, both in time and effort, ongoing research will usually decrease the overall costs, as well as providing a continuous, ready supply of valuable information upon which the business can act. The lead-time in designing, launching, conducting, analysing and drawing conclusions from customer research and surveys is long, and early work is likely to suffer from a lack of experience and understanding. Keeping customer monitoring constantly 'on the boil' requires an attitude of real interest and positive input from senior management, as well as a sensible and practical approach to the research undertaken. However, such a strategy repays any expense, in terms of both speed and the quality of material that can be made available to various parts of the business, and to the Six Sigma quality initiative in particular. The continual, proactive use of customer listening posts through such areas as sales force feedback, complaint analysis and marketing analysis will ensure that the focus is maintained, and that at least one ear is always turned to the customer.

PRACTICAL CUSTOMER RESEARCH

Before approaching customers, it is important to understand fully what is required in the way of an answer. Six Sigma requires many diverse facts and information from customers, and it is not usually possible to gather more than one or two parts of the entire picture at once. Repeated visits to the customer base will be required; this may be a problem when there are few customers in any one segment and a good relationship with such customers must be maintained at all times.

Gathering information

Early visits to the customer base will aim to gather broad information, such as identifying and quantifying core processes. Here, the question will be: 'What matters to you, the customer?' Later, the approach will aim for more detailed answers leading to quantification of exact requirements, and questions will become very much more specific.

Sampling is always a key issue, and a good representation of the customer base is required in every approach. Enough customers must be included from each segment without unduly influencing any particular group either way. Classic examples of poor technique by opinion pollsters over the years abound, but it is highly unlikely that any quality initiative would have to achieve such a delicate and public result from such a large population. Until an organization approaches four sigma or better across all the core processes, error and inaccuracy in customer research is more likely to add a slight bias to the quality initiative than it is to hinder progress or cost money. Many research organizations exist which can either help with customer research or conduct it on your behalf, but the information returned is only likely to be truly useful to the quality initiative if the research organization fully understands what is required. This is unlikely unless it has past experience of Six Sigma, and the costs involved in the repeated small-scale customer research that is at the heart of Six Sigma imply that doing most of the work in-house is often a better solution.

In simple terms, accurate sampling will:

- be based on the objectives of the survey;
- ensure adequate numbers and a random selection;
- take into account different segments to ensure full representation.

Many organizations will already have some form of customer database, but this must be checked thoroughly for accuracy and detail before it is used. If the database is incomplete, inaccurate, insufficiently detailed or just does not exist, then time and effort should be spent in setting one up. In the early stages of a Six Sigma initiative, gathering information from customers will be intrusive, in that the customer is consciously involved in the survey. Organizations which have adopted store loyalty cards have realized the benefits that such schemes bring, and are able to extract detailed purchasing behaviour information without the need to interact with customers in any way.

There are many survey options, which can take the form of a personal interview, focus group, telephone interview or self-completion questionnaire. The *personal interview*, which is ideal for the top slice of important customers, can deliver excellent results, but it is costly and difficult to conduct for street or point-of-sale surveys. *Focus groups*, where a number of carefully selected customers are invited to an 'open discussion'-type meeting, are ideal forums to identify and clarify broad points. Here, trained facilitators are obligatory, as is a neutral setting with some incentive for attendance, and such events are therefore costly to stage. If an organization wishes to find out exactly what matters to customers, then this is almost the only way to gather such information. The majority of basic surveys are carried out by *telephone*, which offers speed and cost advantages, and can easily be completed by the sales department, telemarketing department or an outside organization. *Self-completed questionnaires* are a very low-cost option, are not subject to interview bias, and can be applied to many situations. However, the response rate is both low and slow, and the return sample will be unrepresentative and uncontrollable. *Customer complaints* and *general response cards* offer very little information, and are highly unreliable. Some alternatives to surveys that can provide useful information include self-benchmarking and competitor benchmarking, mystery shopping, sales team feedback and general market research. Such general information can often assist with validating survey results and placing conclusions in a sensible perspective.

An essential issue with any survey is to maximize the response rate. This is particularly important in later stages, when improvement teams will frequently wish to check CTQ parameters or improvement ideas rapidly, using a telephone survey of the absolute minimum number of customers. No survey can be completed in less than about four weeks from start to finish, but sending an introductory letter and perhaps a reminder letter beforehand and making appointments, even for telephone calls, will help improve the response rate. Ensuring there is a named person to contact and also a script to work to is very important. In general, people are quite willing to spend a few minutes on the telephone and little incentive is required, but it is always polite and good practice to follow up any survey by writing back to respondents to give a summary of the results and an intended action plan.

The questions asked must lead towards some conclusion and gather sufficient and appropriate information for sensible analysis to follow. The general rule is to ask about present behaviour rather than past experiences, and to target behaviour rather than attitudes or simple classification. Piloting and testing of surveys is essential, and well worth the time and effort.

Analysing results

Analysis of the results can be carried out manually for small surveys of under 100 respondents, but the use of software (spreadsheets or specialist survey software) can make life much easier. The aim must be to convert the survey output into firm numbers rather than woolly conclusions, and the choice of question style is important. Several different rating scales exist; the most generally

Please read the following statements and place an 'X' in the box which most accurately reflects how much you agree or disagree with each statement.

	Agree strongly	Agree slightly	Neither agree nor disagree	Disagree slightly	Disagree strongly
When checking out, speed is important.					
The checkout process today was fast.					

Figure 4.2 Examples of survey questions

suitable is probably the *Likert scale*, which is based on degrees of agreement with a statement (see Figure 4.2).

It is important to ensure that questions are structured with care to avoid a number of pitfalls. Early questions must be simple and easy to answer, and all questions should follow a logical flow and grouping. Ensure that questions can be easily understood, and avoid ambiguity, unfamiliar words and questions with double meanings or double answers. Questions need to be constructed so that bias is avoided and a true answer obtained; many people feel that they should have an opinion even if they do not have the information necessary to give an answer!

In Figure 4.2, the scale has been balanced with five points for responses. There can be seven or even nine points for finer graduation, but the centre point should always be neutral. Two general issues are being addressed here: firstly, clarifying whether 'checkout' as a process is important, and secondly, gauging how well the process is currently performing. Once the general importance of 'checkout' as a (core) process has been quantified, this question could be dropped. The word 'fast' is subjective, and later this would need to be narrowed down to a more precise figure using different questioning. Asking for the same information more than once can help verify the accuracy of the answers, but again care needs to be exercised: 'I am happy to queue for a checkout', 'Checkout delays are an issue to me', 'If I had to queue longer, I would not mind', and so on.

The output from such a question can be converted to numerical values quite easily, and is normally rated as '1, 2, 3, 4, 5'. The analysis that follows is quite simple, consisting of adding the outputs for similar questions, and then calculating the average, range and statistical deviation. The average is the indicator that is of prime interest, but a high standard deviation of more than about one point can indicate a problem with the results. Cross-tabulation is a powerful tool, and can show trends between similar or associated questions or groups of respondents. It is often helpful to include a general question to close, such as checking the degree of agreement with the statement: 'I am happy with the service provided by this store.' As long as sufficient data points have been collected and there are no fundamental problems with the survey in general, the results from such a question can often be linked back to other questions, thus shedding light on what really lies behind a sense of good service or quality. If other circumstantial or demographic information has been captured along with the question responses themselves, results can be associated back to such things as age, spend, distance from store, and so on.

Drawing conclusions from the results is almost as difficult as conducting the survey itself. It is important that everything is checked back to reality and that nothing is read into the figures that cannot be verified. Surveys are often used, like statistics, to prove a contentious point, and there is always leeway for blaming bad survey technique to discredit unpopular results. No manager who has staked a career and millions on the introduction of a new checkout procedure will take kindly to a survey that proves customers actually do not like it.

DETERMINING CRITICAL TO QUALITY CHARACTERISTICS

Basic surveys and focus groups will identify the outline core processes which are deemed to add value for the customer, and can also provide an indication of their relative importance. From this point, it becomes necessary to determine exactly what are the customer requirements for each individual process, and to set specific target limits. Analysing customer needs and setting associated targets are difficult tasks, and can easily be compromised by lack of stringent vision, time and effort. The entire process must be customer-centric, and it is often difficult for people closely involved with the day-to-day operations of an organization to put themselves in the position of an external customer. Becoming a customer for a day or even an hour can reveal much about the current state of an organization's products and services, as well as strengthening the ability to develop an open attitude and to 'think customer'. Reflecting on the many hundreds of times every week each person acts out the role of customer for one organization or another will also bring home how rare it is for customers to be asked exactly what it is they want from a product or service.

Voice of the customer

Ask a hundred people what they like about their local supermarket, and the result will be an overwhelming medley of qualitative information and noise. Customers often have difficulty in expressing such concepts, and frequently miss the obvious. However, the raw information, often verbatim, can be of more practical use than neatly packaged presentations from professionally engineered customer research. 'Voice of the customer' material comes from focus groups, interviews, market research, complaints and feedback, being a customer, surveys and observation of customers in action. Nothing in this list is particularly outstanding in terms of low costs, lack of bias, value of data or ease of application, and in most cases organizations will have to rely on whatever is feasible in terms of time and effort. The ability to listen to and facilitate expression from customers is the most important consideration at this stage.

Use of the 'what if'-type question can be very helpful to draw out from customers the underlying and unspoken factors critical to the product or service. In general, basic elements such as safety are taken for granted, and customers cannot express an interest in new things for which there is no precedent. Only by suggesting the addition or removal of such elements in products or services can genuine feedback be enticed.

Once an initial question has been asked, it is necessary to probe for a deeper understanding. This may entail re-stating the answer in paraphrase to check for understanding, and then moving off into other related areas of questioning. Requiring respondents to rank their answers either relatively or absolutely imparts some sense of quantification to output data (see Table 4.1). Relative ranking is much easier than absolute.

To determine the importance of shopping trolleys and baskets for supermarket shopping, for example, questioning could start with 'How important are shopping trolleys to you?', which is

Table 4.1 Ranked survey

Shopping trolleys are important for shopping:	(Low)	1 2 3 4 5 6 7 8 9 10 (High)
Trolleys are too big:		1 2 3 4 5 6 7 8 9 10
Trolleys are too small:		1 2 3 4 5 6 7 8 9 10

unlikely to inspire any enlightening responses. Better to ask, 'How often do you use a shopping trolley?' and then move on to 'Have you ever *not* used a trolley?' and 'When do you find trolleys a nuisance?', and so on. Only when the respondent has consciously fully considered all the hidden issues is it possible to ask for a ranking.

Verbatim quotes are also helpful, both for later requirement analysis and to demonstrate the reliability of the findings to the more sceptical, for example:

- 'All the groceries get squashed in the bottom.'
- 'The wheels get stuck and the children can't push them, they are too big.'
- 'The problem is what to do with the trolley when you've finished shopping.'
- 'I really like the small trolleys, they are so much easier to use, but there are never enough of them.'
- 'It's a pity that they can't expand or contract to the size we need.'
- 'The supermarket down the road has some nice shopping trolleys that I like.'

Customer requirements and needs analysis

Moving from the verbatim 'voice of the customer' to firm 'requirements' is aided by the intermediate step of 'key issues'. Looking at the above (fictitious) summary of quotes from a number of customers, it would be possible to say that one key issue for customers is the size and shape of trolleys, and perhaps also their manoeuvrability. From identifying a key issue, the next step is to list one or more *requirements* which, if satisfied, would resolve the issue to the customer's satisfaction. A requirement from the above key issue could be that each customer has access to the size of trolley best suited to their needs.

Requirements are difficult to write, as there are often many variations that ultimately seem to say much the same thing, and yet attack the problem from different angles with differing degrees of success. A good requirement statement for the service industry should:

- be measurable;
- be concise yet complete;
- not be a solution;
- avoid the abstract.

Manufacturing industry has slightly different considerations for such requirement statements. Here, the important drivers are that specifications (requirements) are measurable and actionable, and in themselves are often associated with a finite solution. A manufacturer's quality specification for a shopping trolley would state a certain size and shape, material and finish. Quality has often been stated in such terms of product specifications, and as a result has often stopped short of actually satisfying the (end) customer.

An attempt such as 'Each customer has the trolley most suited to his/her needs' is concise, but somewhat abstract and difficult to measure. What are the needs, and how would anyone know whether they were met? Perhaps, too, the idea of 'shopping trolley' is a solution to a deeper customer need associated with the collection and assembly of goods to purchase. To list some of the needs, such as space or compartments which prevent goods being squashed, or a trolley that is not too big and unwieldy and is easy to manoeuvre, can lead to almost a shopping list of wants, which is even worse.

Sometimes, the issues are easy to identify and convert to requirements. For example:

Voice	'Checkout takes too long', 'I don't like queuing', 'Items take so long to ring up on the cash register.'
Issue	Customer wants no queuing, customer wants fast checkout.
Requirements	Checkout queues are as short as possible, and items are processed as quickly as possible.

In the above, there is no hint of a solution (unless 'checkout' is itself a solution) and the requirement comes in two parts, each of which can be measured with a stopwatch and clipboard. The problem with the shopping trolley requirement is that each customer has many diverse needs that do not lend themselves to being combined into one issue statement. One way of dealing with this is to say that the issue is that: 'Customers want to be able to select a shopping trolley best suited to their individual needs.' A solution would be to provide more than one type of trolley, but this must not be implied in the requirement. A more suitable requirement statement is: 'During a visit to a store, each customer can use a shopping container best suited to their particular needs.' This still leaves abstract concepts of needs and difficulty in measuring success, but this can be overcome by using a customer survey to measure resultant satisfaction. This is not ideal, but it is workable, in that a full requirement statement could be something like:

> On each visit to a store, each customer can have the use of a shopping-gathering container which is easy to use and which they rate as meeting their requirements for such a receptacle – measured by customer survey.

It is so much easier and simpler to say, 'Customers can find a shopping trolley each time,' which is easily measured and very concise (and easy to action – order more trolleys), but does it really satisfy the customer? Recent introductions of a variety of shopping trolley shapes and sizes have shown that customers were never really satisfied with just the one shape and size, and in time the shopping trolley may be eliminated altogether. The real basic need here is for an appropriate device to gather together the multitude of items to be purchased.

If struggling up towards a customer requirement is proving difficult, the alternative is to work down from high-level concepts of general customer needs. Certainly, this is the best approach when designing new products or processes, such as Internet shopping, where nothing currently exists and it can be very difficult to obtain reliable 'voice of the customer' material. Sometimes, a mixture of both approaches is needed, followed by a visit back to the customer base to check that the requirements are appropriate and sensible. It must be remembered that the essential aim here is to arrive at a set of requirements which, if met, imply satisfied customers, and testing requirements on customers is always a good idea. Sadly, creativity and inventiveness are always in short supply when new concepts are aired, as it is easier to work from what already exists than to conceive the new. Many Internet shopping sites use a 'basket' in which goods are placed. This may shield tentative shoppers from the shock of the new, but very rich and important people never use baskets when they go shopping, they just point and have it delivered later. Shopping is an experiential activity conducted for the sheer pleasure, or for the sheer necessity, depending on the viewpoint. Starting at such a high level and working down can shed new light on the real needs and requirements for a first-class shopping experience.

Maslow's hierarchy of needs is a list of human requirements covering the full range, from the basic to the abstract. In ascending order, they are:

1 physiological;
2 safety;
3 social;
4 self-esteem;
5 self-actualization.

Defining the immediate needs of a retail shopper from this list is both difficult and of little practical use in the short term. Shopping for groceries is about meeting a physiological need for sustenance, and doing it at a major supermarket can imply safety, security and value. The social element and esteem come into play too, but this does not lead to firm, measurable and actionable requirements for quality.

A more suitable list of needs, at least for the service industry, would be something like the KARES list:

1 **K**nowledgeable staff;
2 **A**ccess to services;
3 **R**esponse and speed;
4 **E**ase of use;
5 **S**afety in use.

These are general headings, but they can provide a starting point from which a customer-needs tree can be built. 'Ease of use' is of prime concern for a supermarket, and shopping trolleys would fall under this heading. Getting to the shop, parking, hours of opening and so on fall under 'access', and finding items, gathering purchases and paying for them sit nicely under 'ease of use'. Starting from this point of view, it may be easier to arrive at a set of requirements that encapsulate all that is good about shopping. Certainly, a top-down approach makes it easier to avoid dragging existing processes and solutions into the equation.

As Maslow noted in his hierarchy of needs, not all requirements have the same weight or importance. *Kano analysis* looks at the different types of requirements that must be satisfied for customer quality. It had long been assumed that customer needs were one-dimensional, in that the better the functioning of the service or product, the greater the satisfaction, and vice versa. As shown in Figure 4.3, this equates to the one-dimensional straight line relating service functionality with user satisfaction. Noriaki Kano is credited with introducing the idea of 'must-be' requirements, which are absolutes that cannot be left out. Failure to meet this class of requirement less than completely in any way will result in dissatisfaction. Personal safety is an example, almost taken for granted until it is removed from the picture, leading to great distress. To this are also added 'delighters', which are services not expected by customers. If they are not there, no change in satisfaction results. However, by adding in an element beyond customer expectation, the service provider can improve the level of experienced satisfaction considerably. It is very important that the resultant requirement list is graded using this approach, and appropriate action taken. The

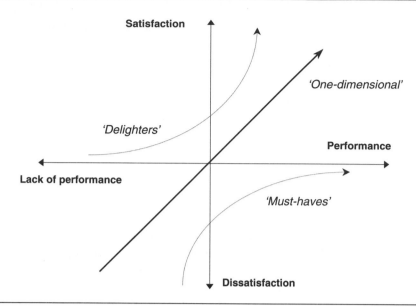

Figure 4.3 Kano analysis diagram

'must-be' list will include safety, integrity, continuity, accuracy and many other things commonly taken for granted. On no account can such requirements be diluted or omitted, since the immediate result will be a definite reduction in experienced satisfaction and quality. The competitive drive comes from introducing new offerings in the 'delighter' range, and ensuring that all the standard 'one-dimensional' needs are met at the upper end of the line. Bringing in new ranges of shopping trolleys will delight those whose needs have not been met until then. However, over time, requirements move from being a delight to being one-dimensional to being a 'must have'. Driver air bags in cars were once a novelty, an extra that added value but did not detract from the basic satisfaction if it was not fitted. Not a firm requirement at first, they soon became a standard requirement, and are now verging on the 'must-be' area.

It should also be noted that people are individuals, not lemmings or sheep. No single person will fit exactly into a standard profile of customer requirements, and for some people there will be a level of indifference to, or even reversal of, a requirement feature. Some people are totally indifferent to the availability of a variety of shopping trolleys, and in some cases such arrangements can actually cause dissatisfaction: there are now so many varieties that it can be difficult to find the one required, and there is no longer room at the front of every store to hold sufficient stocks of each type. A few years ago, a child-size shopping trolley was introduced in some stores, in an attempt to delight parents with young shoppers. Regrettably, the result was usually a few bruised ankles, more work for the parent and store, and something else to block the aisle.

One very powerful tool that is used extensively to design new products is Quality Function Deployment (QFD). The use of this particular tool in both Japan and America has developed almost to a fine art, and it would take an entire book to detail and explain it fully. The basic issue is how best to step or map from a set of identified customer needs to a set of possible features that could be offered to the customer. Nothing is simple or perfect, and for each need there may be many possible offerings, the question being: 'What is the minimal best mix or selection which results in the highest overall delivery of satisfaction?' The simplest form of QFD is a *customer needs matrix*, where identified needs are listed on one side of the table, and possible features are ranged along the top. Each need is ranked by customer importance, using Kano analysis and customer surveys to identify a priority value. Each feature may or may not contribute to one or more needs to various degrees, and by scoring the interaction between 'feature' and 'need', the best minimal set of features can be identified. Such features then become the requirements on which the Critical To Quality characteristics are founded. Table 4.2 shows a set of first- and second-level needs for a mythical supermarket, and the proposed hypothetical features. Suggestions as to how well the features might meet the needs (high, medium or low) have been located on the matrix, and from this a nominal score value can be determined. The score is arrived at by multiplying each interaction rating of high, medium or low by the corresponding customer rating on the left, and then summing all values for that column. The high, medium and low interactions can be represented by values such as 9, 3 and 1, or 5, 3 and 1 – several suggested scales exist, and this is certainly not a precise tool.

Such a table is useful in building Critical To Quality characteristics, and in checking for missing features or features that add little value. The high scores for some features imply that they well meet many important customer needs. Other features may score very low, perhaps implying that they either fail to meet customer needs, meet needs poorly, or meet only low-rated needs. Analysing the completed table can demand as much work and effort as its initial completion, but it does help in the critical appraisal, evaluation and numerical ranking of new ideas in the cold light of day.

Setting target values

The path from customer to CTQ is long and arduous, but the end of the journey will lead to an actionable and measurable characteristic which is critical to customer-perceived quality (see

Table 4.2 Customer needs matrix

First-level needs	Second-level needs		Multiple trolley types	Scanning checkout	Value-item produce	Large stock held	Free-roaming assistants	Extra-wide aisles
		Importance						
Speed	No queues	7.8	LOW	HIGH		LOW	LOW	LOW
	Fast checkout	8.2		HIGH			LOW	
Ease of use	Sensible trolleys	6.5	HIGH					
	Good store layout	6.8						MEDIUM
Accuracy	Accurate billing	9.9		HIGH			LOW	
	Find everything came in for	5.3			LOW	MEDIUM	LOW	LOW
	Value for money	7.5			MEDIUM	LOW		
	Score		66	233	28	31	31	34

Table 4.3 Critical targets and limits

General need	Ease of use
Specific need	Appropriate shopping trolley
Feature	Many trolley types
Critical To Quality	Always a variety of types to choose from
Measurement	Number of trolleys of each type available
Limit	At least 25% of each type at storefront at any one time
Ideal	At least 50% available
Lower	20% available
Upper	100% available

Table 4.3). Each CTQ must then be associated with precise customer limits, which will be used to measure how well quality is met. Setting a limit is again one of the more difficult tasks within Six Sigma, and is particularly so in service industries.

A key requirement is that CTQs are measurable, and that measures can be applied to inputs to or outputs from a process, or indeed steps within a process. For a manufacturer, output quality specifications are normally applied to output measurements, and are explicitly set by customers of the ensuing processes. For example, in the manufacture of tiles for suspended ceilings, there will be an upper and lower limit to the size of each tile: too big, and it will not fit into the framework; too small, and it will fall through it. Setting a limit here may be as simple as coming to an agreement with the manufacturer of the framework. In the supermarket checkout process, there may be several measurements that could form excellent CTQs, and one might be the average time taken per item. Speed and timeliness are both excellent candidates for CTQs, as time is always highly visible in service processes, is easy to define and measure, relates well to the experience of quality, and can often be radically improved. Counts of things are also easy to measure and improve, as are accuracy and availability.

Normally, there is a tension between setting an aggressive target for the benefit of the customer, and a sloppy target for the benefit of the producer. Being honest and realistic about what the customer wants will imply another survey visit to the customer base, and duly accepting the conclusions. Customers probably do not want to queue at a checkout at all, so the ideal target is zero wait time for attention from a checkout operative. The limits in this case will be zero for the lower limit, and about two or three minutes for the upper limit. The saying is true: you can please all of the customers some of the time, and some of the customers all of the time, but never all the customers all the time. Raising the upper acceptable limit improves both current performance and the process sigma metric, and the leeway and ability to improve the process, but it does muddy the water. What *is* an acceptable upper limit?

Figure 4.4 shows a type of survey questionnaire that can elucidate a level-of-service requirement from customers. The results from such surveys will return a range of answers, and setting a finite cut-off point can be very difficult. Traditionally, the 50 per cent acceptance mark has been used, which implies that only half of the customers will be satisfied, even when performance is within limits. Six Sigma quality aims to satisfy *all* customers, and in theory at least, the targets should be set to satisfy everyone. This would mean no queues at the supermarket – what a nice place to shop! Realistically, some loss of performance must be accepted. Genichi Taguchi has

Please show the levels of service you think a *supermarket checkout* should provide by marking each box according to the following key:

U = unacceptable level of service   – mark *all* boxes which show an unacceptable level of service
E = expected level of service   – mark only one box on each row
I = ideal level of service   – mark only one box on each row

	Level 1	Level 2	Level 3	Level 4	Level 5
Time taken to queue for a checkout	Over 5 minutes	2 – 5 minutes	2 minutes	1 minute	Less than 1 minute
Time taken per shopping item at checkout	20 seconds	15 seconds	10 seconds	5 seconds	2 seconds
Number of items failing to be scanned first time	16 in 100	8 in 100	4 in 100	2 in 100	1 in 100

Figure 4.4   Simultaneous multi-attribute level trade-off questionnaire

introduced the concept of a *loss function*, which holds that customers become increasingly dissatisfied as performance moves away from the target. In the example in Figure 4.4, the ideal target is likely to be the best average of all customers' ideal service, and the acceptable limit set so as to include, say, 80 per cent of all indicated acceptable levels of service. Much as it may be wished for, Six Sigma is not (yet) a precise science.

It is as well to remember that targets change over time, and this process needs to be revisited frequently. Also, remember that there are likely to be lower as well as upper limits, even in time-related situations. The ideal time taken to scan each item at checkout is likely to be equal to the time taken to pack each item into bags. Go slower, and customers wait; go faster, and customers feel harassed at the payment stage. Of course, two shoppers together may be able to pack faster than one can, and it may be that several grades of targets and limits are required for different groups of customers or situations. Ultimately, each customer wants what is ideal for them, and for this to be repeated on each visit without variation or loss of performance.

Setting a target is ultimately a best guess; in reality, it is regrettable that the management of customer expectation is often preferred to the odious task of actively pursuing quality improvements. A form of cheating is quite common in situations where external quality measurements and limits have been unwillingly imposed. Local authorities in the UK, for example, are required to process planning applications within a set number of weeks, which is a limit set by central government. General practice is to defer starting the clock until the application has been officially registered, allowing only those applications which can be processed within the time limit to be admitted. Unfortunately, such a policy is folly in a competitive market where others may decide to deliver aggressively above current expectation. If it can be done better, quicker, smarter and at a lower cost, then someone somewhere will.

SUMMARY

- The customer and customer satisfaction are central to Six Sigma quality.
- Customers are both internal and external, and include non-customers (who have gone elsewhere) and not-customers (who have not consumed the product or service). The aim of excellent quality is to increase the customer base by meeting or exceeding customer expectations.

- Critical To Quality factors are measurable and actionable characteristics of a process or product which relate well to customer performance requirements, and thus customer satisfaction.
- To meet customers' needs, it is necessary to identify customers and customer segments, ascertain specific customer needs, convert these into process or product requirements, and then identify or design service or product features to best meet these requirements.
- Determining customer performance requirements involves obtaining 'voice of the customer' material by means of surveys, focus groups, observation, market research, active participation and general feedback.
- Setting CTQ targets and upper and lower limits is generally a subjective trade-off between satisfying a given proportion of the customer base, and appeasing the organization. Realistic but aggressive targets are necessary in a competitive situation, and are preferable to any attempt to manipulate customer expectation.

CHAPTER FIVE

The Vision and Benefit of Six Sigma

If Six Sigma as a quality initiative and methodology is so centred on the customer, what is the possible benefit for the producing organization? We live in a very self-centric and materialistic commercial environment, and few organizations subsist simply for the public benefit. Considerable resistance to change, quality and Six Sigma in general exist even in organizations which have wholly embraced such ideals, and such resistance is partly due to a feeling that it is nothing but hype and a waste of time, money and effort.

Six Sigma, in its entirety, is targeted at the very things that hurt organizations and reduce effectiveness and profitability. Businesses make money by selling added value. More profit is made by increasing the added value, the marketplace and unit sales, and by reducing costs and waste. Many factors influence such matters, including customer perceptions and expectations, employee profitability and loyalty, as well as the product, service and marketplace. It would be folly indeed to claim that a single elixir could cure all ills. However, application of Six Sigma quality has shown over the past decade that claims for its ability to turn water into wine have a substantial grounding in reality.

Here is a roll call of some of the benefits seen by three of the leading organizations which have applied Six Sigma quality amounting to a clear and proven return on investment (figures are taken from a number of public sources, and may not be specifically related to Six Sigma quality benefits alone):

- **Motorola**
  - a 99.7 per cent reduction of in-process defects;
  - a saving of more than $11 000 000 000 in manufacturing costs;
  - a productivity increase of 12.3 per cent each year, on average.
- **AlliedSignal**
  - a cost reduction of $1 400 000 000;
  - price-per-share growth of 520 per cent;
  - a 16 per cent decrease in introduction time for new products;
  - a 24 per cent reduction in the billing cycle.
- **General Electric**
  - net savings of $1 500 000 000 in 1999 from Six Sigma alone;
  - expected eventual annual savings in excess of $6 000 000 000;
  - an average share price increase of 40 per cent each year.

None of the above indicates anything about 'soft' benefits, such as public integrity, market standing and consumer respect. Nor can it begin to show fundamental changes to the very nature of the organization, and the way in which such businesses now move forwards under the corporate umbrella of Six Sigma quality.

TO BE WORLD-CLASS

The companies which adopted a Six Sigma quality approach prior to the late 1990s were principally American multinationals competing in global markets. This pattern will change rapidly over the next few years, as more and more organizations follow suit and adopt similar quality strategies. In the world-wide marketplace of today, competition is fierce indeed, and it is necessary to be world-class to deliver the very best products and services. Japanese producers have learnt how to deliver to a cost and performance level that delights the consumer, and everyone else must either follow and compete on the same terms, or be left behind. With the increasing use of the global Internet for commerce and trade, even small and single-nation companies will need to aspire to world-class levels of service.

Six Sigma as a pure metric is highly achievable, and consumers are able to detect a one or two sigma-value difference quite easily. Aircraft passenger safety is taken very seriously, and flying is currently an extremely safe mode of transport. If the customer measure of success is simply to be able to walk off the aeroplane at the end of the flight, and the opportunity for defect is taken as one air-flight per day, then three sigma implies a failure every two weeks. Four sigma, at about 99 per cent, implies a failure every five months. For cabin crew who fly daily as part of their jobs, even five sigma performance in this area is not good enough, as failures would occur every twelve years or so. Currently, air safety is above six sigma performance, and closer to seven sigma, with failures of less than one in a million. Baggage handling, in contrast, performs closer to the three sigma mark. Air travellers from London to New York experience a likelihood of baggage loss for each flight of around 4–8 per cent.

In October 1997, Jack Welsh (CEO of General Electric) addressed the GE Capital second annual quality reward and recognition seminar, and described some of the very positive benefits that had already been achieved. GE Plastics had implemented process improvements that had delivered savings in materials and final product equivalent to building a brand new plant. This is a twofold benefit: firstly, in terms of gaining the output from a 'virtual plant' that has cost nothing to build and maintain, and secondly, in having the ability to measure such a gain and fully ascribe it to the quality initiative. GE Railcar, which services and repairs American railroad company wagons, had for years provided what was generally considered a good customer service. The quality initiative had shown early on that the average turnaround for a typical railcar service was fifteen days, but the customer wanted it to be only five. Successes by that time had already reduced the turnaround to nine days, with the target clearly set for five days. The dramatic impact that had already been delivered was entirely due to providing the customers with exactly what they wanted. For this organization, speed – time for turnaround – was the key to customer satisfaction, and by delivering to customer and not producer requirements, business turnover had increased by some 60 per cent over the same period.

To be a world-class quality organization implies three things:

- the ability to improve quality in the eyes of the customer;
- the ability to cut waste and costs internally;
- the ability to measure the impact of these improvements and ascribe due credit to the chosen quality initiative.

All three elements are important to a successful quality initiative.

Defect-reduction amounts to hard savings in most cases. For industrial applications, it is easy to see that prevention is better than cure, and zero defects is better than a 'ship and fix' attitude. In the service industry, where the 'product' is often intangible or invisible, such an attitude can be difficult to inspire, and exhortations to 'do it right first time' often lead to increased scepticism. The secret, found long before Six Sigma was conceived, is to change the process so that it is not possible to deliver anything but perfection each time. Such a radical concept does indeed work very well within the service industry: everything is a process, and it can be improved.

Any business sold as a going concern has a nominal value attached to its *goodwill*. This sum purports to make payment for loyalty and continued custom from the existing clientele. It is strange that it is often only when organizations change hands that such premiums are quantified. During the normal running of the business, no account is taken of the asset of a good, loyal customer. Perhaps this is because it is not something that can be sent to the bank, but it is something that must be paid for every time an existing customer leaves and has to be replaced. There is a major cost involved in seeking out and wooing custom. With fierce competition in the financial services markets, research has indicated that for insurance or consumer credit companies, new customer accounts only return an overall profit in the third or even fourth year after commencement. Within the UK mortgage lending market, the rush to acquire new customers by whatever means can only pay dividends with a resulting long-term stay, and early departure spells considerable loss of financial investment in time, money and effort.

To become world-class, customer satisfaction must take pride of place within the aims of the organization, for it is only by doing so that the real benefits from quality begin to turn into hard cash. The realization must come that the customer, the product and service, quality and costs are not isolated areas, but are all interrelated. The real cost to an organization of poor quality is the sum of waste and inefficiency, together with the loss of business esteem and value when customers are dissatisfied. Businesses which lack direct customer contact tend not to consider the entire picture, and to ignore the value of customer contentment.

COST OF QUALITY

Both Joseph Juran and Phil Crosby have written about the cost of quality. Crosby extended the concept by stating that 'quality is free', and it is this principle that counters the additional costs of implementing extensive TQM quality initiatives. Traditionally, increases in quality have only been brought about by incurring additional inspection and rework costs. Such an attitude is based on the narrow view that only the individual defect is an issue. What is important is to be able to add up all the costs associated with bad quality, and to balance them against the new costs associated with the extra quality initiative. Using a total-view approach to costs, Crosby showed that up to 25 per cent of profits were lost to the 'hidden factory' of waste and inefficiency in every plant, and that all these losses could be prevented at minimal cost. Waste is obvious, and elimination of waste by reducing defects can therefore return something like an additional 10–20 per cent of profits in manufacturing. Only by measuring processes accurately and identifying the equivalent 'waste and rework' can service industry also quantify cost savings from the defect-reduction approach.

Study of examples of processes in both manufacturing and services often brings to light a common factor, in that all processes are initially set up to provide a path for the most common passage of an entity. Failures during the processes generally pass to an alternative path, designed to catch the exception or reject. This secondary path is unlikely to be as efficient or well designed, and will certainly involve rework, delay and more expense. Further, it is the exception that proves (tests) the rule, and such 'alternate entity paths' have an increased tendency to propagate further error and omission.

Figure 5.1 is highly simplistic, but serves to demonstrate the point. The principal path A is likely

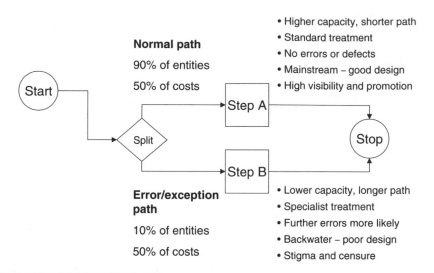

Figure 5.1 'Good' and 'bad' process paths

to have, say, 90 per cent of entities going through it, be they widgets or service instances of one form or another. The alternate path B has only 10 per cent of entities due to an exception or failure. Measurement of such processes can show that as much as half of the overall expended effort and costs goes into the lower path. This is due to a number of reasons, in that this path will require more work and perhaps specialist staff or operations, and will have been less well designed and operated. Putting the house in order and moving only 9 out of every 10 'alternative' path entities can save over 40 per cent of running costs overall.

The value a satisfied customer brings to a business can be much more difficult to quantify. The starting point is to remember that all sales, and hence revenue, are based on the total customer pool. It can be said that profit comes from revenue minus costs, and revenue is related to the number of customers and the average customer spend. More explicitly:

profit = number of customers × (average spend − variable costs) − fixed costs

To increase profit, it is necessary to increase the number of customers and the average customer spend, and to reduce both variable and fixed costs. A large part of this equation hinges on the total number of customers, and Figure 5.2 demonstrates the principles involved. Customer loss is not entirely due to dissatisfaction, but a considerable proportion of it is, and by dealing with the issues that lead to dissatisfaction, the attrition rate can be slowed considerably. Once the outflow rate has been so reduced, the customer pool will begin to increase in size, and also begin to contain a higher proportion of better-satisfied customers. New customers are, in part, brought in by recommendation, and the arrival rate will also therefore increase. Costs associated with retaining loyalty can be reduced, as can the costs associated with obtaining new custom. Further, higher satisfaction will lead to a greater spend and more frequent repeat spends, and decreased operating costs and higher staff moral. Nothing is more invigorating than satisfied customers and the goodwill they bring.

Quantifying this is difficult, but can be achieved by knowing and understanding the customer base, by surveying customers and conducting disloyalty analysis. Not-customers and non-customers are crucial to such work, and will aid identification of the main reasons why customers

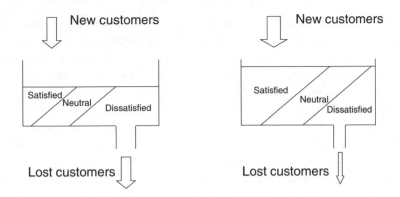

Figure 5.2 Increasing the customer pool

leave, or do not join in the first place. Associating this with the identifiable customer pool turnover will place a rudimentary figure on the potential revenue each extra customer can give, and the potential gained from increased satisfaction. For service industry, a rough figure would identify an extra 15 per cent of profits gained for a 5 per cent increase in customer numbers.

Cost savings are less difficult to identify, and generally easier to associate with defects. Figure 5.3 shows how total revenue spent on process entities can easily be summed and apportioned. Calculating the savings is then simply a case of multiplying defect reductions by the decrease in costs the improved process has delivered. Here, one step has been removed altogether, all three other steps have had cost savings applied, and the two steps with rework have had the defect rate reduced. It is always a good idea to benchmark such defect-associated savings against the initial state at the beginning of the quality initiative. As time goes by, the number of defects will reduce, and the apparent savings to be gained will become smaller. Driving any quality improvement simply by counting defects and cost reductions will stall at around a four sigma level, as the further reduction in the total defect count will amount to less than 1 per cent, and the total possible savings that could be made will have also been cut. Pushing any improvement further requires a much broader viewpoint that considers defective *units*, rather than just defects.

What customers really want are products and services without blemishes or faults of any kind,

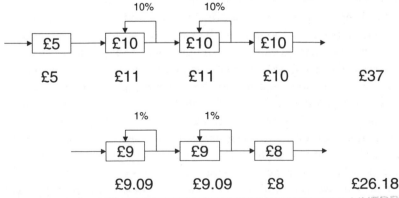

Figure 5.3 Process step cost savings

together with consistency in the delivery of such products and services. The lowest cost and effort for the consumer implies an ability to purchase goods or services with confidence, and be able to justify repeat purchases from the same supplier. Not only do customers dislike failure, they also dislike variation and inconsistency. The major chains of fast-food outlets have grown market share as much due to the guaranteed delivery of an identical product each time, every time, as they have due to the added value of the product itself. Consumers do not, in general, like to take risks with purchases, and this implies that variation and the unexpected is highly unwelcome.

The author's recent experiences as a UK customer of domestic white goods indicate that even where defect rates are low, the complexity of modern appliances leads to failure for the customer far more often than is expected. A washing machine with a purchase price of £250 has failed twice within the first year, leading to the need to replace an inlet valve and drum bearing. In itself, each failure is apparently rare, but the costs associated with the defect are considerable, and this customer will not be repeating a purchase from that particular manufacturer in the future. Often, failures do not account for the customer-side costs, which generally amount to a lot of time, effort and worry. A large domestic refrigerator purchased from a highly reputable manufacturer developed a defective light switch. The total direct costs associated with this switch are probably no more than a few pence to make it, since it has only three metal and four plastic parts. The costs involved in fixing this defect were the sum of a call to the service centre, the stocking and dispatch of a spare part, and the time and support costs of a service engineer. Of course, nothing runs quite that smoothly for the exception, and three return calls to the service centre were necessary to arrange and rearrange a suitable and convenient appointment. Then, on the first visit, the switch was declared not to be at fault, and a repeat callout was required when it failed again one month later. This time, the stock control department had dispatched the engineer with the wrong type of switch, so a third callout was required. The total costs probably amounted to in excess of £50, measured in terms of the producer's time and resources. The costs to the customer are almost immeasurable (including three half-days off work), but have supplied the material for countless dinner party conversations at the expense of the manufacturer. Loss of only one customer purchase in future would consequently amount to a loss of profit for the manufacturer, and then a further loss of goodwill that a new and satisfied customer could have brought. Saying that the switch costs 50 pence and that there is a failure rate of 1 per cent, so losses are 0.5 pence per unit, misses the point. The purchase of six major items for a new kitchen has resulted in three items requiring a total of seven service calls in the first year!

Service industry is no exception to the above situation – indeed, the goodwill from satisfaction is much more likely to pay in the long term than are cost savings from a reduction in defects. Physical products, by their nature, have an extended time and monopoly with customers, and there are greater costs associated with cutting losses and moving to another brand. Services tend to be short-term, both in duration and memory, and switching is so much easier. The real costs associated with a defect in terms of supermarket checkout involve the time spent by the cashier, which can be small with the use of modern scanning cash registers. The issue occurs when customer dissatisfaction spills over into disloyalty, as it so easily can in this circumstance.

Turning cost savings into real money is not always straightforward either, as it will involve cutting out real expenditure. A change to a manufacturing process one week can easily return hard savings the next week, in terms of a reduction in raw materials and processing. Service processes are far more complex, often use little in the way of 'raw materials', and hard cost savings may not accrue for many months. If raw materials can be removed from a service process, real savings can be realized immediately. If the process can be shortened, then the staff involved can either be moved, removed or reallocated. There may be many thorny issues associated with staff removal or reallocation, and it may be better to aim for an increase in future capacity rather than reduction of overheads. By installing new checkouts, a supermarket may be able to process customers twice as quickly as before. The temptation exists to do away with half the checkouts and staff, but this leaves no real benefit for the customer (or staff), as the queue will be just as long as before. Retaining a customer-centric viewpoint on cost savings implies that a slight reduction in the number of checkouts, particularly at quiet times, will benefit both consumer and producer. The added value that this new process could bring lies in being able to increase throughput at peak times, and yet still meet customer requirements. This will ultimately lead to increased customer satisfaction, and hence greater customer numbers and profit. In the long term, the issue must be to retain the market lead; far too many businesses begin a slow decline in customer satisfaction by being victims of their own success.

More and more organizations today are realizing the benefits associated with outsourcing parts of the enabling processes. The core processes are the ones that add value, so they are the ones that should be concentrated on. Enabling processes need to be highly efficient, and handing such work over to outside organizations can lead to increased opportunity to realize real cost savings. There are fewer moral and internal objections to reducing the expenditure with a supplier of goods or services than there are in undertaking redundancies among one's own staff. A reduction in the defect rate of refrigerator light switches will only return a real cost saving if, firstly, it affects the customer-perceived defect rate for the whole refrigerator, and secondly, if service call costs can be reduced on a pro rata basis. A more modern, and perhaps enlightened, approach to business process re-engineering is to aim for an aggressive target for growth, and thus to match service improvements from quality projects with increases in business volume and revenue. Here, key drivers for cost savings will be aimed at reducing processing costs per entity, and future cost-avoidance rather than short-term staff reductions.

Associating savings with quality projects and CTQs is also fraught with issues, as it can be difficult to relate impact to reality. It is useful to commence at the very top, with a list of key CTQs that ultimately drive customer satisfaction, and then to apportion revenue changes and cost reductions to items in this list. Certainly, holding a total overview at a very high level is one essential element to directing the quality effort to where it can best return real profit. Another essential element for satisfactory results is to ensure that specialist financial input and resources are available throughout, and that processes are in future driven with one eye on cost savings and revenue increases, to ensure that expected savings actually turn into reality. Good financial returns can be made in the short term from 'quick-hit' process improvements, and thereafter, further return generally only materializes when the opportunity for cost savings is converted into reality. The big savings are elusive, and will only begin to show when all aspects of the quality initiative begin to come together. Finding the select few critical factors that wholly and directly influence customer satisfaction, and then delivering to these right across the board under tight control, will ensure a handsome return on the effort expended.

WORKING WITH CUSTOMERS AND SUPPLIERS

As quality initiatives move beyond simply reducing defects, and on towards delivering low-variation and defect-free products and services, it becomes necessary to change the way processes are monitored and controlled. Rather than monitoring just financial and business functions, it is more appropriate to monitor the customer-oriented core processes, using the key CTQ characteristics which define acceptable customer quality. Such monitoring also needs to ensure that the business targets and requirements are met, by monitoring volume, revenue, profit and costs, and also internal CTQ measures. Enabling functions also need quality improvement initiatives, and will likewise need to be monitored for ongoing efficiency and performance, but such measurements are often directed inwards to the business, not outwards to the customer.

The concept of a *dashboard* has been introduced in order to monitor such important quality and associated process measurements effectively. Like its equivalent in a motor car, such a device brings to the observer a summary of the overall performance, together with key indicators that monitor specific and crucial measurements. A process dashboard will include performance indicators such as volumes and revenue, as well as process sigma metrics for the CTQ measurements. The use of control charts and other Statistical Process Control tools can be complemented by measures of such factors as the number of customers and customer complaints and so on, which add realism and common sense to what can otherwise be mere facts, figures and graphs. If an organization has set long-term targets for defect rates, customer satisfaction or volumes, then current performance against targets can easily be indicated using 'traffic lights', which show green for 'on target', amber if there are issues outstanding or expected, and red if targets are compromised. It is also possible to combine multiple process sigma metrics together, by loading each value in proportion to the number of opportunities for defects, or by the customer-perceived value of each CTQ. Using the formal definition 'defects per million opportunities relate to the ratio between *total* number of defects and *total* opportunities' allows a 'global business' sigma process metric to be calculated, although other approaches may be more realistic in some situations.

Dashboards are excellent devices for use within an organization, and can generate considerable pride, motivation and positive internal feedback. In embarking on a Six Sigma quality approach, all employees soon become actively interested in the process sigma metric for their particular processes, and for the organization as a whole. Once the idea of dashboards has been introduced and developed, an organization may see benefit in publishing such results from the quality initiative outside the business. Most companies will have a handful of critical major customers which lead both demand and revenue. By sharing progress results with such customers, the link between excellent quality delivered and that experienced can be reinforced, enhancing the relationship with them. This idea can be further extended by inviting customers to be more practically involved within the quality initiative itself, and to even direct where future efforts are best placed. It is, of course, the customer who best knows what constitutes good quality in terms of products and services, and the customer is best placed to both benefit from and judge the results of any quality initiative.

The use of a quality *scorecard* has been shown to provide excellent feedback, both for the customer and for the organization. Each scorecard contains a simple rating for perhaps one or two CTQ characteristics which matter most to one customer. The customer is invited, on a regular basis, to score or mark the organization in terms of these measures, and both customer and business monitor the results closely. Each scorecard must be tailored to one customer, so general and widespread use is often not practical. Further, it is unwise to place more than one or two CTQs on any one scorecard, as the result is likely to be a poor response to dealing with several low scores in the short term. Setting up a scorecard requires some time, as it is necessary to agree with the customer both what is to be measured, and how it is carried out and ultimately scored. Results are often limited to quarterly judgements, so it may take almost a year to set one scorecard running. Once in progress, it is to be hoped that there will be a steady improvement on the customer score, and care needs to be taken to ensure that the quality effort is both present and able to deliver such improvements. The *balanced scorecard* is a recent development as a tool for monitoring corporate progress across areas of customer, operational-process and employee development as well as the more traditional financial indicators. Although called a 'scorecard', it is an internally generated monitoring aid, and the author prefers to use the term 'dashboard', reserving 'scorecard' for measurements generated (or scored) by external agents such as customers and suppliers. Whatever it is called, a balanced scorecard (dashboard) has much to gain from a Six Sigma approach, which monitors customer, employee and operational processes through CTQ measurements.

The long-term benefits from scorecards are extensive, and they can become one of the tools an organization uses regularly to ensure that CTQs are kept up to date, and targets and limits are accurate. There is also no point in hiding one's light under a bushel, and customers are more likely to take notice of improvements over time if they are actively encouraged to look for them.

Such long-term customer partnerships can also be extended to suppliers and beyond, to the benefit of all. It is not a good idea to insist that external suppliers to the organization meet Six Sigma standards. Many believe that Six Sigma is not possible in practice, and imposing such a burden is not likely to be at all acceptable. However, sharing the rewards of a first-class quality initiative such as Six Sigma can include making staff who are expert in Six Sigma quality, and associated training materials, available to suppliers and customers themselves. All processes interact with suppliers and customers at the start and end points, and where such processes go beyond the boundaries of the immediate organization, considerable inefficiency can lurk. In general, it is not good practice to extend the quality improvement effort past any point where an organization has control, impact or jurisdiction. However, where such an extension is clearly in the best interests of both parties, it can be encouraged.

When transacting with others, it is often assumed that the other party aims to win in the transaction at our expense. In response to this, many defensive mechanisms are introduced to counter such a threat, and even turn the balance of the transaction the other way. Such attitudes can add considerable wasted effort, and even lead to real loss of business, even in the simplest of cases. Organizations often distrust customers, to the point that custom is made more difficult than it should be (or even impossible). For example, invoices are often written with the assumption and slant that the customer will not pay. Non-payment is not usually in the interests of the customer either, so such efforts are at best wasted, and at worst insult or hinder payment. The spirit of Six Sigma means that in such cases, the organization should actively go out of its way to help the customer pay. Safety and self-protection from deliberate harm are still vital to any organization, so this does not mean dispensing with credit controls, quality checks and suchlike. However, the ability to distinguish between necessary safety and unnecessary distrust can lead to the removal of stifling controls which merely add to transaction costs. If a supplier of component parts has undertaken output quality control and assurance, why introduce similar input quality control and assurance processes? The failure of quality assurance must surely be that it offers no real guarantee that customers will actually be satisfied. By using Six Sigma quality to bridge the gap between supplier and consumer, both organizations can fully agree on one joint CTQ characteristic, and by setting up a common scorecard, at least one party can remove an unnecessary quality assurance step. Symbiotic relationships exist quite frequently in the real world, and the efficiency so delivered underpins a transaction that might otherwise be too expensive to complete.

The spirit and vision of Six Sigma is to deliver constant and outstanding performance in the eyes of the customer. To seek this in earnest will ultimately involve removing the artificial barrier that exists to define 'you' and 'me'. In service-related processes, true quality often only comes when action is taken to make the process really work for the customer, not (just) for the business.

SUMMARY

- Real benefits can be gained from a quality initiative aiming for world-class quality in terms of:
  - reductions in process defects;
  - savings in process costs;
  - increased profitability and shareholder value;
  - improved customer satisfaction and esteem.
- To drive better quality, it is necessary to balance the costs involved. Traditional added inspection and rework should be avoided by eliminating defects and reducing variation from processes in the first place. Increased profits come from lower costs and an increased customer base, driven in part by an increase in customer satisfaction as a result of fewer defects and greater consistency.
- Increased profit results from:
  - a larger customer base, because (a) growing customer satisfaction will lead to a reduction in the loss of existing customers; (b) products and services will be more attractive, with fewer defects; (c) capacity and capability will be increased, and markets will be wider; (d) new products/services will be delivered to the marketplace more quickly, and (e) there will be greater numbers of new customers due to referrals from other satisfied customers;
  - lower fixed costs due to reduced overheads;
  - reductions in variable costs by (a) removing redundant process steps; (b) lowering process step costs and increasing efficiency; (c) reduction in the overall number of defects, and (d) increasing capacity as a result of reduced variation.
- Real cost savings can only be made by eliminating raw materials, and reducing time and effort or expenditure on outsourced supplies or in-house resources and services. Future savings are made by constraining existing operating costs while increasing capacity and productivity.
- Further savings can be made by working more closely with suppliers and major customers to reduce transaction costs. The use of dashboards to monitor internal progress and improvement, and scorecards to facilitate customer-driven quality, will lead to new levels of benefits.

CHAPTER SIX

Implementing Six Sigma in Practice

Implementing a Six Sigma quality initiative principally involves a radical and cultural change in the way an organization thinks about itself and interacts with its environment. There are technical and practical differences, such as the way processes and functions can be managed and controlled by CTQ measurements, but the greatest single change will be a transformation in the attitudes of all the employees. Many varieties of quality initiatives have been applied in the past, and current vogues lean towards accreditation in international management standards such as ISO 9000 or similar. A common 'knee-jerk' reaction within the service industry when faced with visibly poor customer service is to send all staff on a customer-service training course. In general, 'all staff' excludes anyone in management, and the training amounts to little more than role-plays and pep-talk lectures designed to encourage a more positive attitude and enthusiasm. There have indeed been a number of times when such exhortations to do better have produced results, but success is never guaranteed, and often little visible change is evident just a year or so after such courses have taken place.

Six Sigma alone is absolutely no guarantee of success, and a number of organizations have already experienced what amounts to a failure in implementing it. Any company wishing to make substantial gains in any area of business needs both a strategy and a game plan. Six Sigma quality is no exception, and because it is all-encompassing, the strategy and plan must permeate every corner of an organization's structure.

THE STRATEGY OF QUALITY IMPROVEMENT

Firstly, it is important to quantify the main reason for embarking on a new or fresh quality initiative. If, as is most likely, an improvement in shareholder value and company profits is the fundamental reason, then this should be borne in mind and stated from the outset. Just as Six Sigma embodies a visible goal within the approach, so must the Six Sigma quality initiative have its own goals and targets, and these should be clearly stated from the beginning. Implementation of Six Sigma is not a goal in itself, but part of a larger plan, and the ultimate goal should be incorporated within a mission statement, such as:

> We aim to double shareholder value over the next five years by aggressively improving all aspects of customer service using a Six Sigma quality approach.

Perhaps a doubling of shareholder value is of little interest to most employees, but such tangible goals are possibly better than aiming for a six sigma process performance across the company in five years, and better still if motivation is backed by company-wide rewards tied to share value.

Once a mission statement has been devised, the next step is to ensure that objectives and targets are set. The mission statement above actually includes such a target, and can therefore serve both purposes. Using Six Sigma as the quality initiative provides the main tactics through which the objectives will be reached, and all that is then required is a strategy plan for the implementation.

It may be tempting to compress the entire Six Sigma quality initiative into less than a four- to five-year span, and even allowing for the fact that much work has already been done to understand and develop Six Sigma quality as a concept and methodology, this will indeed be a stretch. In living through such a compressed execution, it can be easy to miss fundamental contributors to success or failure, but speed does give the advantage of being able to rapidly assess, assimilate and adapt, and the following is an outline of the various stages to be expected within the overall strategy:

1 preparing;
2 launching;
3 learning;
4 improving;
5 mastering.

Preparing for Six Sigma

In order for major (and particularly cultural) change to have fertile soil in which to germinate and ultimately blossom, there must be an openness to alternatives, together with an internal structure that can rapidly alter, grow and adapt. Most current management patterns slide slowly but inevitably towards the 'big company' attitude, where tight fiscal controls and tiered management structures stifle inventiveness, adaptability, change and growth. Any Total Quality Management implementation is as much about changing attitudes as it is about changing processes, and attitude-change needs to start with management and the inherent company structure.

The introduction of Six Sigma to General Electric has been very successful, in part due to early preparations during the 1990s that were aimed at bringing back the 'small company' attitude, and increasing employee empowerment to act and cut through bureaucracy. Productivity drives and 'best practice' followed, actively encouraging the search for better ways to do things, even outside the primary organization. This enabled a more proactive process-improvement strategy, followed by the introduction of a 'change-acceleration' technique, designed to facilitate cultural change and change-acceptance at the fastest possible rate. No matter how good the proposed technical improvements are, the final results depend on general acceptance of the associated required change. More refined strategic initiatives then followed, facilitating better quality, increased globalization and a more rapid introduction of new products and services to the market. The final step before introducing Six Sigma was to actively involve customers by passing winning techniques on to major clients through joint initiatives and workshops. This has the dual benefit of internally enhancing the importance of the customer, and forging stronger links with important clients.

It is advisable for an organization to likewise first test and then improve change-acceptance by introducing a strategy of lesser importance not directly connected with Six Sigma quality. Bringing in external consultants with new ideas, fresh approaches and different agendas may not lead directly to amazing proactive change, but it will at least break up hard and stony ground and identify areas of resistance and scepticism which need to be dealt with first.

There are a number of reasons why change and quality generally die within organizations, and past experiences from proponents of TQM have noted disappointments because of:

● poor vision and planning;
● lack of management commitment and a real change in behaviour;
● little involvement from all staff, and cultural conflicts;
● few measurements to gauge TQM improvements in the long term;

- change-management and process improvement not working together;
- over-zealous bureaucracy stifling quality management;
- no long-term commitment to ongoing quality improvements.

Six Sigma deals excellently with the issue of measurements, but there is nothing in a pure Six Sigma approach that insists that senior managers must get involved and change their behaviour. Certain essential elements in any change programme are required as enablers and facilitators, and Six Sigma is no different. There are certain areas where any organization must ensure genuine strength before launching any Six Sigma initiative:

- training;
- communication;
- resources;
- planning;
- commitment.

Because of the complexity, extent and depth of a Six Sigma approach, particularly in service industries with no history of Statistical Process Control, *training* is an essential enabler for the promotion of the knowledge and new skills required. *Communication* must also be highly effective in all directions, up and down, and may require a fresh approach to listening to and empowering others less used to being heard. Meetings, and lots of them, are commonplace in dynamic organizations that are going places, and this in itself can be a barrier to success if people are not familiar with, accepting of or adept at such practices. Any initiative also requires *resources*, and Six Sigma can be exceedingly hungry in terms of the time and effort required across the entire organization. Modern management practices in some companies devote 10 per cent of working time to quality in general, even once a major initiative has settled in. From a purely logistic point of view, a Six Sigma initiative is a major undertaking, and *planning* and project management are vital to facilitate, monitor and control every aspect of the roll-out. Finally, *commitment*, both in the short and long term, is vital. Any hint that the new initiative is merely a passing fad will become self-fulfilling, and organizations where management says one thing and does another will certainly see little long-term success. Actions always speak louder than words!

Launching Six Sigma

Six Sigma is about a *common* metric and approach to quality, applied and working across an entire organization, through which *everyone* has the same clear vision, goal and tools by which customer satisfaction is to be improved through excellent quality. Many aspects of this approach therefore militate against a diluted or piecemeal implementation, particularly the heavy statistical basis and (somewhat regrettable) set of nomenclature that have come from the Japanese and American influences. Trial launches, part-launches and a 'toe in the water' approach are almost certainly guaranteed to lead to problems, will not return the benefits expected, and are therefore not to be recommended. Rather, what is needed is a massive, single launch that generates sufficient momentum to overcome the inevitable initial scepticism, and carries everyone in the organization through to the next stage. This implies real planning and effort, together with all the necessary input, resources and a high profile to ensure that the whole company can move forward together.

In Europe, early hesitancy towards Six Sigma has arisen from the distinct American flavour, and possibly the inability of American (parent) companies to fully appreciate and react to the cultural gap between America and European countries. Even within Europe, many cultural and practical differences abound, and sensible organizations will realize that what works in the UK will not necessarily work in France, Germany, Denmark, and so on. Six Sigma remains very much an American quality concept, both in word and deed – a fact that must certainly hinder its uptake elsewhere. Training must be readily available locally, and provided with due regard for language and cultural needs.

It is perhaps a good idea from the start to have a *Business Quality Council* (BQC) in each locality, drawn from local senior management, key business leaders, quality leaders and any external agencies supporting the initiative. This council can take responsibility for ongoing planning and direction, and for ensuring that all other necessary enabling resources are in place.

The launch period itself is perhaps best considered in terms of the local practice for a general election. In the UK, such events are well publicized, follow a well-understood tradition, and ensure good communication to get the message across. They also ensure involvement and active participation from all, including the voters. Party workers actively canvass and distribute manifestos, and major figures deliver speeches, debate on television and radio, and go out and meet the people and kiss babies. Obviously, not all of this is vital for a Six Sigma initiative, but the essential differences between the UK and US electoral procedures highlight the underlying cultural differences between the two countries. In the USA, employees were exhorted to become 'lunatics for quality', and some people were even observed wearing T-shirts emblazoned with 'I am a quality lunatic.' Care must be taken to ensure that the medium does not detract in any way from the message, and the Six Sigma message should be locally adapted and presented in the best possible light (hopefully, without diminishing the content in any way).

Learning with Six Sigma

No matter how much experts say and teach about Six Sigma at the launch, the real learning is to be found in the doing. There are literally hundreds of reasons for failure in any quality and change initiative, and only by running Six Sigma quality projects and process improvements will exponents develop a deeper understanding of exactly what is involved, and how best to apply both theory and practice. As well as the structured application of a Six Sigma methodology, there is an art to applying Six Sigma, and such an art takes time to learn, appreciate and act upon.

The learning stage is the time following launch, when the first improvement projects begin and run to completion and Six Sigma must prove itself. Such initial projects need to be nurtured and protected to ensure highly visible success, and such success must be carefully measured and appraised. The real return from hard savings, adapting Six Sigma principles and techniques to the local organization, and overcoming initial hesitancy and scepticism is of considerable worth. To arrive at such a goal, initial projects must be selected carefully to ensure that they are feasible and can rapidly return visible and guaranteed results. Nothing contributes quite as much to long-term success as success itself.

Early projects should be few in number, be based on the critical and central core processes, and should involve staff who show early enthusiasm and solid empathy towards Six Sigma, as both a vision and a methodology. Publicity should be extensive, ample time and resources should be made available, and rewards for contribution and success should be endowed in a high-profile fashion. This is also an excellent time to conduct more general benchmarking across the entire organization, and to promote general tools such as process mapping and customer surveys through wider training. Early customer surveys are unlikely to return specific information useful to current and later projects, but increased customer contact will begin to develop the principle of customer-centric service that is to come. This is also the time to develop customer databases and other tracking tools for later use. Information technology and computer systems will play an important part in providing measurements and supporting changes from the improvement stage, and financial support will be needed when developing cost and saving models to quantify the value of process improvements. Key staff from such areas should be actively encouraged to work on early projects, and can be included in cross-functional process improvement teams.

Improving with Six Sigma

Once the entire organization has begun to grow familiar and comfortable with Six Sigma, real progress can then be made. Early investment in general Six Sigma awareness training, and the involvement of many staff from across the organization, will spread both ideas and enthusiasm to every corner. Training, which can place major demands on resources, can now continue according to a pyramid approach, with staff who have been trained early, and perhaps externally, now delivering training internally. Motivation must be maintained, and newsletters, events and company-wide refresher training can all help to reinforce the message that Six Sigma is not just a passing fad.

Having established a blueprint for the local initiation, roll-out and support of quality projects, the frequency and duration of such projects can be improved upon so that change now spreads to all areas of the business, and can begin to include enabling functions as well as core processes. Inevitably with such a major initiative, certain areas may have been overlooked or not received the full attention deserved, and this is a good time to measure the effectiveness of the Six Sigma message. A new or reinvented quality department driving Six Sigma should be accountable for the correct application of tools and concepts. Strong leadership must continue from the top, ensuring that Six Sigma delivers to the overall strategy plan and targets. It has proved worthwhile in practice to strengthen the value, uptake and practical spread of Six Sigma by ensuring that all expert quality staff are trained and certified, and that all executives are required to complete a certain level of training and to conduct a quality project on their own.

Other secondary benefits from the quality initiative should also begin to bear fruit at this stage, and positive feedback from employees about changes in management, a more open and honest structure, better communication and a stronger sense of belonging, empowerment and worth should be sought and encouraged.

Mastering Six Sigma

As Six Sigma is such a conceptual change from past ideologies and has a very recent pedigree, only now are some of the finer points beginning to emerge. Diving into process improvements to return immediate cost savings is very possible (and highly laudable) for the majority of organizations, but as time passes and improvements begin to settle in, a natural ceiling for process improvement seems to be reached. There is good reason for setting earlier statistical controls at approximately three to four sigma. Under normal circumstances, plain enthusiasm, drive and grim determination can quite easily deliver at a four sigma level of performance and, with care, can sustain this level over time. Going beyond this, however, requires much more than simply repeating the cycle of improvement time after time.

For complete success in Six Sigma, the ultimate goal is perfection, or at least as close to it as is humanly possible. At this extreme edge of capability, where processes repeatedly and consistently deliver failures at less than 3 parts per million, old rules have to be replaced by new philosophies and practices that can genuinely deliver such outstanding performance. Human error rates will ultimately limit process delivery to about four sigma, or a 1 per cent failure rate, and going further and yet remaining profitable often requires new processes carefully designed and founded upon technology. Up to about four sigma, organizations will mainly concentrate on improving existing processes based on existing principles and practices. Going beyond this point requires new processes that need to be designed with a six sigma capability built in, generally by using new technology that is harnessed productively. Typically, it is the application of new technology and recent technical advances that drive new levels of performance in any field, but technology always brings its own problems. The mastery of Six Sigma requires that process development and process improvement are driven by sound business requirements, based on customer needs and applying the best available technological initiatives. The 'design for six sigma' approach naturally evolves from and is an extension of the simpler 'improve for six sigma', but it is as well to learn to walk before trying to run.

As processes move closer to six sigma, the visible financial returns will decrease. Very few organizations (particularly non-manufacturing) actually generate over one million opportunities for a defect within a year, and defect costs are likely to be small. Under such circumstances, deploying large-scale quality project teams is like using a sledgehammer to crack a walnut. The paradigm for customer-driven quality must be extended even further to counter the apparent diminishing financial returns, and the application of Six Sigma quality must evolve to higher levels. The Japanese quality movement still continues to make strides forward in this respect, as *kaizen* quality becomes more a way of life than just part of a job or task. There also exists the trap wherein driving Six Sigma quality endlessly forwards can move an organization into a tightly bound state where inventiveness and creativity are wrung out of its day-to-day operations through quality standardization and overly rigid control. Here is a paradox: to reduce defects and variation for the customer, organizations must add defect and variation to themselves, to allow 'ordered chaos' to give birth to fresh ideas and inventiveness.

Of course, the mastery stage never ends, as Six Sigma is more like a journey than a destination. Like painting the Forth Railway Bridge, once the process is complete, it will again be time to revisit all the CTQs, and to adjust the targets to ensure continued competitive advantage. Six Sigma is indeed a journey that is hard to start and has no end – finding the inner strength and will within an organization to stay the course is the secret of long-term success.

PROCESS IMPROVEMENT PROJECTS

The more ethereal a concept, the more difficult it is to apply and maintain any sense of pace and enthusiasm. Six Sigma quality does at first seem highly daunting, if not an impossible task, and it is imperative that the practical application is combined into one easy-to-use process. Early attempts to divide quality improvement tasks into easily achievable chunks arrived at a circular process, based on a project, of:

- plan;
- do;
- check;
- act;
- plan ... and so on.

This holds much value, as it recognizes that improvements are generally best implemented as circular tasks that are planned, carried out, tested for results and then followed up with adjustments and perhaps further work. In Six Sigma, however, the 'do' part must be further divided, and many variations on this theme have been developed, and still are. Certainly, there is no 'right way' to conduct a Six Sigma quality initiative in practice, but most approaches exhibit a common thread in the use of cross-functional business teams completing one quality project at a time.

The value of conducting process improvements using teams and projects is well understood, and is at the core of a typical TQM application and the tools deployed therein. Teamwork is common in Japanese companies, and actively encouraged in large, multinational American organizations. Perhaps as a legacy of team sporting activities from schooldays, general teamwork is often falsely assumed to be more effective than the sum of the individual parts. If total reliance upon project teams for process improvements is set to continue, then many organizations will simply not have the resources to be able to use TQM and Six Sigma generally. What can a team provide that one person cannot? The factors include:

- safety and weight in numbers;
- moral support;
- a multitude of skills and knowledge sets;
- ready-made committees and meetings;
- interaction and debate;
- scope for chaos and division.

There is no doubt that a group of people can and does add more value to process mapping, brainstorming and other such team-related tasks. Teams are also excellent ways to quickly spread new ideas and training across organizations, as is required in Six Sigma, and also ensure representation and feedback from a wide audience. In the early days of a new quality initiative, the use of publicly visible teams can help emphasize the importance and value attached to the concept by senior management, and can also help overcome pockets of resistance through weight of numbers. Teams also help to open up management practices, and can begin a subtle shift in control and power that the organization may be looking for in the long-term strategy. Conversely, the overheads involved in running teams are considerable, and much time and effort will be required in early training and support. Team management is a subject in its own right, and early success or failure of any quality initiative can depend almost entirely upon the mastery of building and maintaining excellent teamwork.

Quality improvement is a major task, and like all such uphill struggles, it is best to divide the whole into more manageable chunks, each with a recognizable goal. The climb to the summit of Mount Everest is always undertaken in a series of stages, with base camps and support camps dividing the climb into sensible and achievable sections. The entire organization can easily be divided into core processes and enabling functions, and then each such process can be divided according to key customer measures. Once individual CTQ measures have been identified, and perhaps prioritized, improvement projects can commence on one area at a time, with a goal of moving the processes forward in stages. Ideal early projects are those where improvements are likely to be easy and will return benefit to both customer and the bottom line. Any CTQ involving speed or accuracy in such areas as customer service, billing, ordering, and so on can be a suitable candidate.

Practical improvement in a Six Sigma project is likely to be around a one sigma increase, or a reduction in defects by 90 per cent. Such figures are only approximate, but are suitable and practical business targets to aim for. In starting at about two or two-and-a-half sigma, each project cycle can then move forward to three, four, five and then perhaps even six sigma over a period of about five years. Typically for service processes, improvement projects take between three and six months, and generally cannot easily be repeated at less than yearly intervals, to allow time for the new process to settle in. For processes limited by inherent capability at less than six sigma, incremental improvements are not going to work in the long term, and new processes will need to be designed with inherent six sigma capability. Such work will always involve major projects, taking perhaps several years in extreme cases, but with a two sigma increase or better as a payoff. In internal enabling functions, it may well be suitable to allocate projects to a single person, but this will require an established and effective support and mentoring structure, and good buy-in to Six Sigma across the organization. Such one-person projects can be actively encouraged within an organization once the early stage of the quality initiative has proven itself, and executives can be required to complete one individual project as part of extended training and their career path. As well as ensuring that management learns at first hand how hard such project work actually is, this is also an excellent way to multiply the number of projects completed. Consider a business (unit or local group) with, say, six core processes and ten enabling functions, having only three key CTQs for each. Assuming that one project can improve on one CTQ at a time and move it forward by one sigma, if each CTQ starts at a two sigma performance, this amounts to 192 projects in total to achieve six sigma across the organization. If a more realistic short-term aim is four sigma across the company, this still amounts to almost a hundred projects.

A FIVE-STEP METHODOLOGY

With so many quality projects to complete, it is vital that the process improvement methodology used is both effective and practical. Traditionally, TQM has not been seen as a precisely defined methodology, which must lead to a degree of failure, both in use and uptake, over the long term. The more difficult a task, the more well defined the methodology needs to be, and everyone benefits from having a series of neatly listed sequential steps and actions. Six Sigma still has many areas where choice and use of tools are open to practical interpretation, but the overall methodology does fit very neatly into a sequence of well-defined stages.

Six Sigma, at least in part, is about *measurable* TQM, and early implementations of Six Sigma evolved by first measuring key characteristics, then analysing the results, followed by implementing improvements, and finally, ensuring ongoing and measurable control. For manufacturing, where measurements and process control are highly familiar and part of the daily routine, this amounted to little change compared to the Japanese–American practices in existing TQM approaches, the essential difference being the use of the sigma metric and goal in the 'measure' and 'analyse' stages. Service industry and commerce are radically different, and when the Six Sigma concept first reached non-manufacturing organizations, some alterations to this model were deemed necessary. The principal element added was a *definition* stage, introduced to avoid many of the issues that at that time were seen arising elsewhere, and after initial practical use, a more robust implementation has evolved and is now generally deployed. Figure 6.1 demonstrates the stages and main steps of a typical Six Sigma process improvement in action.

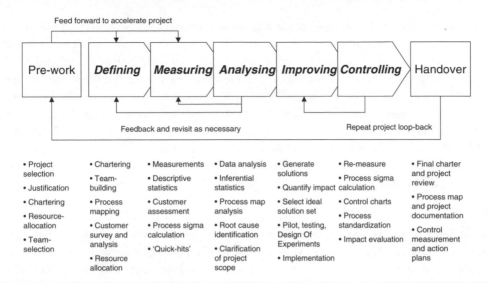

Feed forward to accelerate project

| Pre-work | *Defining* | *Measuring* | *Analysing* | *Improving* | *Controlling* | Handover |

Feedback and revisit as necessary   Repeat project loop-back

• Project selection	• Chartering	• Measurements	• Data analysis	• Generate solutions	• Re-measure	• Final charter and project review
• Justification	• Team-building	• Descriptive statistics	• Inferential statistics	• Quantify impact	• Process sigma calculation	
• Chartering	• Process mapping	• Customer assessment	• Process map analysis	• Select ideal solution set	• Control charts	• Process map and project documentation
• Resource-allocation	• Customer survey and analysis	• Process sigma calculation	• Root cause identification	• Pilot, testing, Design Of Experiments	• Process standardization	• Control measurement and action plans
• Team-selection	• Resource allocation	• 'Quick-hits'	• Clarification of project scope	• Implementation	• Impact evaluation	

Figure 6.1 Typical improvement methodology

Pre-work

Pre-work is not generally part of a quality improvement methodology, but it is required to identify and clarify which projects would be suitable. Suggestions and proposals need to be checked for viability, impact, the availability of resources, strategic fit and expected overall return. The effort expended at this stage will return a dividend, and material can usually be fed into the later stages of the project to accelerate progress.

Project selection is a matter for the business, and preferably the Business Quality Council. The choice and range of projects at early stages in the quality initiative will be limited, and each project needs to be justified fully in terms of all the criteria deemed important to the BQC. Identifying suitable projects will demand considerable shrewdness concerning the overall business, customers and probable CTQs, as well as a sound strategy plan. Early work on process mapping, customer survey and process measurements and analysis will add considerable practical knowledge and backing to any selection. As always in Six Sigma, fact-based decisions are much better than conjecture and supposition.

Once a suitable project area has been identified, an improvement team needs to be launched and allocated initial resources. Each project should be set a target CTQ and a well-defined area to work in, and a suitable sponsor from the business should take overall responsibility for the project, team and outcome. Using sponsors or champions from the area of the CTQ is preferable, and ideally, such a champion should also be the person to whom the final, improved process will return. If the long-term strategy is to shift from a functional business structure to a customer process structure, then the champion will become the new process-owner in the new order, and care in appropriate selection is of paramount importance.

As the champion represents the business point of view, so the project team needs to represent the customer point of view. Whether the work is being carried out by one person, a group or even several teams in succession, they must be independent of the champion. The best way to ensure maximum freedom but accountability is to draw up a *team charter*. The watchword for Six Sigma project teams is 'accountable independence backed by appropriate resource', and issuing a team charter conveys very well both the spirit and practical meaning of such answerable autonomy. Charters can be drawn up by the BQC with support from the quality department and Six Sigma experts, and then negotiated with the intended champion. Requiring the champion to seek the necessary resources and to gather the individual team members from across the business reinforces their involvement and accountability. In action, quality project teams are likely to roam well outside the champion's own area or department, and will certainly require support from across a range of business functions. Only by championing the cause at the top of the organization will the sponsor be able to grant passage without let or hindrance, and in time each champion will be approached by other champions similarly seeking help for their own projects.

Define

The launch of a project team will depend much upon the prevailing Six Sigma understanding within the organization. Early project teams will need extensive training, which can be combined with the 'launch' and 'project review' points. The best way to start a project is to review the charter, and gain its acceptance from the team. The charter is a living document that sets out the roles, responsibilities, goals and aims of the team, together with the accountability and such powers as have been granted by the champion. In the early stages of the project, the team will conduct process mapping, initial customer survey and assessment, and a more formal definition of the CTQ and customer limits to be improved. Working together like this, both team and champion mould the charter to the point at which everyone is clear and in agreement about what is expected and where the project is heading. Discussions should take place and any disagreements should be aired at this stage, not later in the project, when a change in direction could waste months of effort or even cause delicate projects to collapse completely. The 'definition' stage is also a very good time for the team to begin the process of learning to gel and work together before work starts in earnest.

Project charters should embody most, if not all, of the following points:

- business reasons for completing the project;
- a statement of the customer 'problem';
- goal statement for the project;
- boundaries for the project's scope;
- roles and responsibilities of the team;
- outline customer information and CTQs.

At the 'definition' stage, it is vital to identify more formally the customers of the process in question, and to divide the customer base into relevant segments. Customer surveys take time to complete, and may very well run into the next stage, but establishing an early outline view of what matters to the customer, what constitutes a defect opportunity and a defect, and the difference between various customer segments is critical. Exact targets, goals and limits can be difficult to set, and teams are often reluctant to agree precise figures until the 'measurement' stage has identified what might be possible. It is important that aggressive targets are set which represent true customer desires realistically, rather than poor targets that dilute the initial impact of the quality initiative and will not stand the test of time. The use of benchmarking tools at this stage, and a comparison with direct and possible future competition, will often show the need for a major improvement in customer targets.

Each project stage can end with a formal review or 'tollgate', at which point the team, champion, quality and business leaders review progress and direction, make suggestions and perhaps impose requirements before allowing the project to proceed.

Measure

Collecting measurements is a vital, difficult and often time-consuming stage, particularly for non-manufacturing industries that are unfamiliar with the many issues and pitfalls. The reasons for taking measurements at this stage are to:

- add facts and informed weight to the project;
- enable an initial process sigma metric to be calculated;
- provide valuable information for later data analysis.

Only that which can be measured can be controlled and improved. Identifying key measurements associated with the process in question is normally a balance between what would be nice to have, and what is possible to obtain. One crucial measurement will be the CTQ characteristic itself, from which the process sigma metric is to be calculated. Alongside this, other characteristics will have to be measured in order to build a factually based picture of the process and customer, and to aid the later identification of root causes for variations, defects and process problems.

The task of measuring is complicated by the difficulties of gaining information, correct recording and logging, and appropriate data analysis. To ensure that sound data of appropriate value is collected, the team will need a data collection plan, outlining what is required and formal definitions of how to collect it. The collection period must extend over sufficient sample points to ensure that all possible aspects of variation and customer segmentation are included. For manufacturing industry, this should cover various shift and operating patterns. In service industries, weekly and monthly time periods, various offices and branches, customer segments and so on need to be considered.

For example, in a supermarket checkout where the CTQ is defined as 'time taken to complete the checkout process', a project team will obviously have to measure the time taken to complete checkout for a sample of customers. It may also want to collect data about each customer, such as age range, number of items, total spend, branch, operator, and so on. From such measurements, the team can highlight the magnitude of the problem, for example showing that it is the high-spending customers who experience the worst service, and hence the importance of the project to the business. The initial benchmarked sigma metric for the process will also come from knowing the total number of opportunities for defect (checkout events), and the total defects (failed to complete checkout within the CTQ time), or by calculation from the distribution plot of all checkout-time measurements.

Sampling is an important issue that is often mistrusted by teams, and a census rather than an intelligently collected sample can lead to an excessive quantity of data to process and analyse. Manual data collection is very open to error and abuse, and visible measurement always affects the process being studied. The automatic and invisible collection of continuous data, rather than the manual and visible collection of discrete data, is much to be preferred. In the early stages of developing a Six Sigma initiative, however, the completion of projects is far more important than correctness, and good results tend to be gained even with poor execution. This is not to say that bad practice can be allowed or even encouraged, but that strict adherence to statistics may be neither necessary nor appropriate in building early acceptance and understanding of Six Sigma.

The output from this stage of a project should be a collection of well-presented data sets, some of which have already been analysed and described by simple statistics. Information gleaned should be used to reinforce and modify the team charter, and perhaps add support to any quick-hit solutions that may already be visible from the earlier process mapping. While it is important to go into such projects with an open mind, and not to home in on assumed solutions, obvious errors can be corrected once the measurement stage is complete. For example, data may have shown that a particular type of checkout computer system does perform badly, as was expected but had never been proven by hard evidence. This may lead to an immediate decision by the champion to act. It is also at this point that the team will learn for the first time the current state of the process in terms of the sigma metric, which can often come as a shock to all!

Analyse

As Six Sigma aims to be a scientific and repeatable improvement methodology, the 'analysis' stage must focus on facts and reality, rather than guesswork and fiction. The principal objective is to arrive at the set of root causes of poor quality which, due to excessive variation and poor operational control, lead to many of the customer defects. The equation that governs the behaviour of the customer CTQ can be stated as:

$$Y = f(x_1) + f(x_2) + f(x_3) + \dots$$

Y is the CTQ characteristic which matters most to our customer: time taken at checkout, for example. This Y is made up of a series of factors – a function $f(x)$ of a particular variable – each of which contributes in some way towards the final outcome. In a process that exhibits many defects, these factors may be highly random and excessively large, and the desire is to eliminate unnecessary factors, reduce variation and control the behaviour of the rest to fit within the defined customer limits.

The aim must be to arrive at an estimate for an equation that best describes the behaviour of the process. Only when the main factors have been identified will it be possible to change the process sensibly and appropriately, and so improve performance. Inferential statistical analysis, together with consideration and practical analysis of the process map, are the tools used to lead to the identification of root causes. In most time-related service projects, defects are often caused by delay, and it does not take advanced analysis to identify what these are. Delay at supermarket checkouts today is caused by such factors as scanning failures and leaky food containers, which any team should be able to identify simply from observation. The scientific approach implies that the team should go on to quantify both the occurrence and magnitude of such instances, together with the impact they have on the final outcome. Where statistics comes into its own is in hypothesis analysis. By measuring, for example, the time for checkout and the number of items in the basket, such tools as regression and correlation can identify that the checkout time is perhaps causally related to the number of items. Of course, this is obvious, but such careful analysis can often demonstrate the quite unexpected, such as when a greater number of items actually leads to a shorter time, contrary to popular belief. It would not be surprising to learn that the longer the queue, the shorter the checkout time. Armed with such information, a process improvement team can now begin to adopt the role of a detective and start to ask 'Why?' Why should checkout be quicker when there is a queue? If it can be shown beyond doubt that more items in the shopping basket leads to a longer checkout time, the next step is to ask 'Why?', and to keep on asking until a fundamental reason is reached. It may seem utterly worthless to question such a fundamental point, but the answer is that every item has to be scanned. Why? Well, that is the way it is done. Why? ...

Perhaps more interesting is the point that checkout time is related to scanning errors. Why? If sufficient and appropriate data has been collected, stratification and other techniques may point to a greater incidence of scanning errors by junior staff. Why? Poor staff training, perhaps. Alternatively, perhaps labels have been badly printed in the bakery department. Why? The printer is never cleaned. Why? Because it is no one person's job. Why? ... By drilling down past such symptoms of failure, eventually the real root causes for the ultimate defects can be identified, and with care, quantified. Using the Pareto principle, commonly taken to imply that 80 per cent of the problems are caused by only 20 per cent of the root causes, the big issues can be skimmed off the top, ready to be solved and improved.

Improve

Until this point, it is to be hoped that the team has worked with an open and enquiring mind, actively seeking out the principal and genuine reasons for failure. From now onwards, the team needs to actively generate, select and then implement effective solutions that will eliminate such root causes.

Generating solutions is not as difficult as it may seem, and by this stage most teams are working together and are keen to get down to finally fixing the problem. TQM has traditionally used tools such as brainstorming to come up with many ideas, some of which are taken up. Six Sigma improvements still need a few ideas, but the meticulous execution of this methodology can often lead to such a well-defined set of defect causes at this point that the answers are almost blindingly obvious. If the greatest factor in the total time taken to pass through a supermarket checkout is the number of items in the basket, the answer is simple: reduce the number of items in the basket. If 60 per cent of customers buy milk and butter together, sell them as one item. If milk is often purchased in twos, double the size of each item. An oft-quoted example is the bank where, many years ago, a TQM team was examining the issue of the time customers had to wait for attention from a teller. One suggestion was that the money should be left in a pile by the door, and customers could just help themselves. This idea ultimately led to the first automated teller machine.

Given the right environment and active encouragement, teams will often come up with lots of good ideas, and the next step is to apply a cost-benefit analysis, and identify a smaller set of solutions to actually implement. Knowing mathematically how much each root cause affects the CTQ offers the distinct advantage that each solution can be associated with a quantifiable number of defects. The solution-set can then be mixed and matched to give the desired expected improvement level against total cost and effort. Implementation will depend upon the individual circumstances, and in some cases the quality project work can be halted at this point and be handed back to the sponsor. At early stages in a Six Sigma initiative, however, teams will be able to identify many simple but effective solutions that they themselves can implement in a matter of weeks. The use of piloting and Failure Mode Effect Analysis (FMEA) will ensure that the new 'solutions' are not going to make matters worse – something that has a very bad impact on morale, if nothing else!

Where teams are implementing solutions directly, project plans and contingency plans should be used in all but the simplest cases, and for very complex changes, specialist help and assistance may be required. It is likely that the information systems department will be required to make some changes, and this can often be a bottleneck and source of frustration for both parties. Asking the IT department to change, test and install adjustments to the checkout scanning software in three weeks is likely to cause consternation. Resistance to change is an issue that can undo even the very best-executed project, and every team will need to anticipate probable solutions in advance and actively engage in change-management and facilitation right from the start.

Control

Once solutions have been implemented and have become effective, Six Sigma as a quality improvement tool can now reveal its ace card as the team moves into the 'control' stage. Simply by repeating some of the measurements taken earlier, the new behaviour of the CTQ characteristic can be identified and the process sigma recalculated. Process improvement is directly measurable on this common sigma scale, and since the CTQ has been chosen because of its direct relationship to customer quality, the organization can therefore measure the improvement in customer quality and satisfaction.

If, for example, the process CTQ has improved from two sigma to three sigma as a process metric, and if this CTQ is rated as being 13 per cent of overall customer quality, then it can be deduced that for this project and process:

- the defect rate has fallen from 31 per cent to 7 per cent (approximately);
- over three-quarters of the process defects have been eliminated;
- three-quarters of the costs associated with bad quality have been saved;
- overall customer quality has improved by more than 9 per cent (by overall ranking).

No one drives a motor car with a notice in the front saying, 'Think quality – drive safely.' It is not possible to measure 'driven safely' directly, but rather the vehicle speed is taken as the major CTQ metric for road safety. Each vehicle therefore has a speedometer, and allowable speed is specified, monitored and carefully controlled. Likewise, in any organization, process improvements must be measured and controlled if any sustained performance is to be expected. Ongoing process control demands setting up a permanent method to collect and chart the CTQ measure, and a process action plan to ensure that performance is at least maintained, if not improved. Control charts are excellent tools for detecting subtle shifts and changes in a process due to *special* causes of variation. Natural causes of variation are inherent and expected, and different causes of action need to be taken with each.

Figure 6.2 shows a typical simple control chart where some 30 data points have been plotted over the course of time. Considerable changes exist from one point to the next, but this is to be expected and is quite usual, as the data has come from a process 'in control' and exhibiting the expected normal distribution. Statistical Process Control relies on the fact that for normal variation, 99.7 per cent of all outcomes are distributed randomly within three standard deviations (sigma) from the mean. If a data point falls outside this range, or if the distribution pattern is not random, then special (non-natural) causes are likely to be at work in the process, and it is no longer nicely 'in control'.

There are many types of control chart, discussion of which is beyond the scope of this book, but the simplest chart will plot the mean, together with two control lines approximately three standard deviations either side of the mean. Tests can be applied to the plotted points to indicate:

- long-term shift in the average;
- spread due to an increase in the standard deviation;
- non-random behaviour patterns, such as one-off failures or trends.

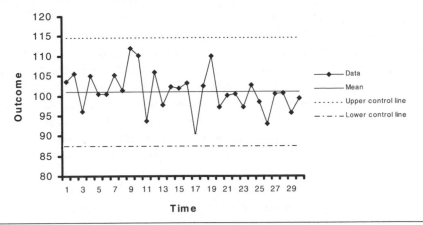

Figure 6.2   Example of a control chart

deviations indicate that

If any of the above are observed, then action needs to be taken to identify what is happening, and why it is happening, and then to do something to deal with the root cause. Such control is very much a departure from typical management of non-manufacturing processes, where if any measurements are taken at all, they are usually fiscal, and control action is erratic and based on more subjective indicators.

Much confusion arises from control charts and the use of three sigma, and the question often asked is: 'Where does Six Sigma fit in?' The *control* lines on the chart are set at approximately three sigma either side of the observed mean, and are used to detect changes away from the current and expected normal distribution. In Six Sigma quality, the goal is to ensure that the mean is centred between the *customer limits*, and that the distance between the mean and these limits is six sigma. If, in this example, the customer limits (which, for simplicity, are not marked) are 100 and 120, then this process is still nicely 'in control', in that it is normally distributed and not affected by special variation. However, such a process has about a one-and-a-half sigma process performance, as half of the data falls outside the customer limits. For this process to be at a six sigma quality performance, the mean would need to be at 110, with the standard deviation being no more than 1.7. Further, if this were the case, it would still be possible for the new control chart to show the process as 'out of control' if points fall outside the three-sigma control lines. Long-term Six Sigma quality performance requires two things:

● that processes meet customer requirements;
● that such processes are stable and run 'in control' without special cause variation.

The role of the team during this stage should be to document fully the project and the improvement changes made, standardizing any new organizational procedures, and to set up a new monitoring and control procedure. It must then hand the process back to the champion or new process-owner, who will take ongoing responsibility for the process and its performance. The project should also be evaluated fully, and the financial gains accounted for and documented. There are likely to have been several solutions that were not implemented by the team, and the scope of the project may also have changed during its execution. The new process-owner, together with the BQC, can make future decisions to perhaps repeat the project or spawn new projects, as appropriate.

CHAMPIONS OF QUALITY

The success of quality projects, and thus of the entire quality initiative, depends heavily on the quality champion. In small organizations, where perhaps a family atmosphere still exists and one entrepreneurial person drives both the business vision and operation, it will not be difficult for such a person to promote a change in direction and marshal resources. This sole person is the best choice to actively promote and facilitate the entire quality initiative. As organizations grow in size, management structure becomes more defensive, and people build walls around business function-ality to limit undue outside influence and protect self-interest. Co-operation between functions is reduced, communication restricted, and apathy and cynicism set in as change becomes more and more difficult to promote and achieve. Driving a new quality initiative from the top downwards will take a long time to change management behaviour, and will be stifled by bottom-end scepti-cism. Similarly, driving the new initiative from the bottom upwards will simply meet resistance as teams try to solve cross-functional issues without the necessary freedom and support. Projects suffer, results are poor, and the new initiative falters without producing the expected results.

Six Sigma project team champions need to come from the heart of the organization, from senior management, and need to both empathize with and understand the Six Sigma vision and methodology. Ideally, the ultimate driving force for the introduction of Six Sigma will still be the very pinnacle of the organization (the local managing director), to whom such champions answer. In successful Six Sigma organizations, the launch and impetus of the Six Sigma quality initiative owes almost everything to the person at the top. In General Electric, Jack Welsh has treated Six Sigma as a personal crusade, and has taken every opportunity to reinforce the message that this initiative is the biggest ever undertaken, and is here to stay.

If it is the person at the very top who proclaims the vision and direction, and if it is the ground-force from the organization who principally enact Six Sigma, then it will be the champions who daily live out the reality of Six Sigma by their actions. Above all, champions need to be confident and have strong self-esteem, which will allow their vulnerability to show and permit others to contribute. By far the most important and successful driving force in ensuring that champions support Six Sigma is the allocation of performance-related salaries and bonuses tied to quality improvement results. Faced with such materialistic motivation, even the most die-hard sceptic will publicly laud quality, and when all voices chant the same song, there is little room for dissent. However, actions speak louder than words, and a perfect champion of quality will demonstrate many characteristics and behaviours, such as:

- holding a vision of customer-driven quality;
- leading, not commanding;
- actively wanting to improve and change;
- measuring processes, not people;
- enhancing communication;
- empowering people to act.

Sometimes, this can be almost too much to ask. The reason why process improvement ideas fail to be generated and developed naturally outside TQM initiatives is that organizations are not normally run with such a culture of openness and change. Allowing – even encouraging – staff from the sharp end of the business to nurture ideas through to implementation is a big upheaval, as control is taken from management and handed over to others who are perhaps not usually deemed capable of making sensible and far-reaching decisions. Asking a person who has controlled a single process for ten years or more to simply step aside and let staff from other departments tinker about is a considerable demand. Insult is added to injury if the team then makes small changes that show more improvement in six weeks than has been seen in six years. People who have been accustomed to manipulating, controlling and even ruling by fear are not likely to change overnight. Perhaps for this reason alone, it is not unknown for organizations to supplement the quality initiative with an agenda to bring a new style of manager to the organization. The career path for senior management can often be via graduate-entry accountants, serving time across divisions, countries and functions. In launching Six Sigma, it may be necessary to introduce an entirely new or radically revised function: a *quality department*, supported by first-rate staff all drawn from the rank and file. The long-term strategy is that such people will in turn become the champions of tomorrow, and will lead the organization with a new perspective and attitude based on continual change and customer-driven Six Sigma quality.

Change culture and management

The pace of market-driven change increases with time; products and services that satisfied customers yesterday will soon become the harbingers of discontent tomorrow. One certainty is that customers, markets and requirements will alter, and for any organization to remain healthy, organic growth and responsive change are basic necessities. In sharp contrast, basic human nature is to adopt habitual patterns and unconsciously resist change, and where structure and tradition bar easy alteration, a culture of no change and stagnation becomes the norm.

There can be no doubt that employees in organizations often question the sense of pointless processes, inefficiency, waste and error. Bad customer service is unpleasant for the staff as well as for customers, but it can often be almost impossible to drive proactive and productive change right through to a successful conclusion.

Change and change-management is not just about culture and attitude. Practical steps can be taken to improve the effectiveness of any change, and such methods are particularly useful to assist the quality teams at all stages of a project. It is *people* who resist change and cause problems, not inanimate objects. Rules and tradition generally dictate ongoing behaviour patterns, but assumptions based on past experience also lead to uncertainty and negative reaction. To overcome passive or active resistance to change, it is necessary to work with people, remove fear, uncertainty and faint-heartedness, and to replace this with a more positive vision of improvements ahead. Change requires effort and adjustment, and often the *status quo* is quite comfortable compared with the short-term upheaval involved.

A visible reason for change

In general, only rebels and youth want change for no apparent reason; everyone else quite rightly expects a sound rationale for change and upheaval. Starting any change initiative therefore initially requires a public vision of the necessity for change, and of the ultimate goal. The reason behind the need for change will start the momentum and begin to drive change forward, and the vision of the changed state ahead will show the direction. It is not sufficient to drive major change simply because it looks like a good idea, or perhaps because it may work better. Everyone who has an interest in both the change and the outcome will need to be convinced by reasoned and rational argument. Here, Six Sigma helps, in that the early stages of a quality project collect valuable data about customer satisfaction, loyalty, and process performance and delivery. Such information can easily help to build and add weight to the business case for the project, and for the necessity of the improvements the team wishes to implement.

Everyone who has an interest in the change process should be identified and benignly assessed to determine their attitude towards the required change. Such attitudes will range from active resistance through indifference to active enthusiasm. Ideally, all the major stakeholders will be positive in attitude, and no one with any major influence will actively oppose the change. Either the team or specialist staff with the necessary authority, facilitation and negotiation skills should attempt early on to influence negative stakeholders using facts, figures and reasoning. It is also an excellent idea to spread the influence more widely, as there is safety in numbers, and rumour and discontent can easily explode without warning. The use of newsletters, information meetings and simply going to talk to people helps inform, enthuse and dispel worry and concern. Keeping the vision going is also important, and regular updates help everyone involved build a positive picture of the new changed state and the benefits it will bring. The early use of external consultants or disparate staff with personal experience of quality initiatives to personally promote the benefits of Six Sigma helps considerably. Nothing is a more powerful agent for change than a passionate, plausible and personal witness.

Facilitating change

Once the change process has been cajoled into movement, every obstacle to the smooth path of progress must be removed. Resistance to change comes only from people, but change in itself deals with both inanimate objects and real human beings. Alterations to processes and procedures will require new materials, machines, measurements, working environments, methods, and even staff. Creating a brand new customer call centre, for example, will require working space, new telephone systems, call-management programmes, computers, answering procedures and scripts, and trained customer service staff. However, if someone forgets to order the new chairs, not only does the progress slow up, but the tide of enthusiasm and excitement can ebb. To carry change through smoothly requires excellent timing and project control. Ideally, at each and every turn, every person involved with the change initiative will find all that they need in terms of resources and facilities to hand, without want or hindrance.

Sometimes, major change can be just one step too far, and sensible compromise is often a sound alternative to patchy success. Better to complete a project well with 0.5 sigma improvement than to push for a full sigma improvement with the possibility of public failure and future change-reversal or a slip backwards. A Six Sigma quality initiative is about a continuous and steady move forward; small and sure steps each time will always lead to continual progress and improvement.

Maintaining motivation for change

It is important to keep the progress of change flowing. Six Sigma quality is not likely to be the ultimate goal in itself, as an organization seeks rather to instil a culture of change and process improvement. Cultural change is about people, and it is vital to place a human face onto any TQM initiative to ensure that it will last.

By monitoring the changes closely and providing reward and recognition for improvements, both in processes and in attitudes, the cycle of change can be reinforced and maintained. The measurement of change is difficult, and by using the quantity and individual impact of Six Sigma quality projects to gauge change and quality, effective progress can be both recognized and tracked.

SELECTING THE STAFF

The skills and knowledge base required for any TQM initiative are extensive, and Six Sigma adds a whole new range of desirable attributes for its practitioners. In general terms, skill areas can be divided into *promoting, facilitating, participation* and *support*. To this end, a fairly typical hierarchy of quality-involved staff will be found in the larger organizations:

- champions and promoters;
- experts and coaches;
- full-time practitioners;
- part-time practitioners;
- everyone (else).

As has been discussed earlier, the champions and promoters of Six Sigma need to come from the top of the organization, and to have the authority and ability to drive the vision of customer quality. Below or alongside these people are the experts who hold the knowledge base required to execute Six Sigma in full. The nomenclature adopted in the early development of Six Sigma has endured, as one principle of Six Sigma is that a common language and metric is used throughout an organization. Such experts are often called *Master Black Belts*, and have a role akin to that of an internal consultant, acting as a change agent. Within organizations adopting Six Sigma, such staff are trained and expected to be experts and exponents, teachers and trainers, coaches and leaders, facilitators and diplomats. The entire knowledge-set for successful Six Sigma quality is extensive, and includes both wide-ranging technical and interpersonal skills. People who can demonstrate depth over such a broad range are rare, and sit at the very top of a large, pyramid-like structure.

Full-time practitioners of Six Sigma are generally called *Black Belts*, and work from within a quality department to support and enable several quality projects at a time. Typically, each project team will constitute a leader and four or five others to provide the necessary roles and skills. One Black Belt in the team will ensure that meetings are organized and run effectively, and that the necessary technical work is completed correctly. As long as such practitioners have the resource of an expert to hand, the need for a full and extensive knowledge base can be avoided. Part-time practitioners have been called *Green Belts*, and have normally completed the work expected of a Black Belt, but perhaps only for one simple project. Employees drafted into a quality project team are unlikely to need a full understanding of the finer details of Six Sigma, but it is good practice to ensure that everyone in the organization both understands and has experience of the basic principles involved. This ensures general support for the quality initiative, as well as a base from which to draw team members and future quality staff. An extension to the 'Black Belt' concept has led to Yellow Belts and Blue Belts, but this is perhaps taking things too far!

In practical terms, each business unit will often require the following:

- a Business Quality Council, including the senior manager, senior business leaders and the quality director, all of whom need to understand Six Sigma concepts and practices;
- champions from the senior staff, preferably covering all processes and functions, who each have an understanding of and empathy for Six Sigma;
- technical experts of Six Sigma quality (Master Black Belts), at a rate of about 1 in every 200–400 staff (or one in each business locality); such people can also be quality managers or directors, and will require several weeks of specialist training;

- quality support staff (Black Belts), at a rate of about four to six to every one Master Black Belt; such people can usually each support four to six projects concurrently;
- team leaders and team members from across the business; such improvement teams require three to six staff, and can run for three to six months (perhaps less for manufacturing projects); the recommended amount of time allocated weekly to the quality project is two to seven hours per person.

From this, it can be seen that the resource requirement is extensive. Early on, such staffing figures can be diluted, and one or two experts can take on most of the roles. Strong emphasis on results from any quality initiative will dictate the need for many projects, each returning quantifiable savings and increased revenue. Early savings need to be made to justify the costs involved in setting up such initiatives, and for later increases in the number of employees who will be directly involved.

WORKING WITH QUALITY ASSURANCE

Quality assurance and international quality standards such as ISO 9000 have gained a considerable following, particularly in larger companies within Europe. The aim of such standards has been to control quality by promoting rigid and well-structured management systems. In themselves, such standards often have little or no direct connection to the customer, and cannot guarantee that products or services will actually meet customer requirements. Indeed, there is likely to be little spirit of customer quality embodied in a control system that dictates repeatability for its own sake. If appalling products and services can and do come from such qualified organizations, what use can these standards be to either customer or organization?

Total Quality Management is far more rewarding than standardization or assurance alone. However, such accreditation may be dictated by both suppliers and large customers, and any previous work from process mapping and documentation will greatly assist with the initial Six Sigma undertaking. Use of standardization and documentation is an essential part of the control mechanisms put in place following process improvement, and should be encouraged to the full. Such control is most definitely best used to support the TQM initiative rather than direct it, and having an existing quality department engaged in ISO accreditation also provides a ready-made structure from which a new Six Sigma quality department can form. At present, there are no universally acknowledged accreditation bodies for anything that amounts to Six Sigma quality, and it may well be that this will never change. Six Sigma is about customer satisfaction, and over time the goal-posts for what constitutes satisfaction will always move. As Six Sigma is more an ongoing journey rather than a goal to be reached, it does not lend itself to an award for achieving any particular target. Perhaps there will be an award to indicate that the organization has reached a state where such excellence in customer quality is inherently possible, desirable and actively sought after.

In time, customers themselves may give out the rewards for excellence in quality. Indeed, one of the best ways to monitor the success of Six Sigma is to constantly poll customers and suppliers to seek plaudits.

EXAMPLES OF SUCCESSFUL SIX SIGMA IN PRACTICE

This section will describe just three examples of Six Sigma quality teams, taken from a range of projects conducted over a two-year period. Although each individual business unit is different, there are considerable similarities between the core processes, particularly with regard to billing, invoicing and payment allocation. Once a particular area had undertaken a quality project, it was possible to 'blueprint' the work, and thus accelerate similar projects in other areas and business platforms. By also working across a pan-European platform, it became possible to run similar projects concurrently or sequentially in different countries, with highly positive feedback and inter-action between teams. Both the similarities and differences found highlighted many aspects of the work, and good use was made of identifying and implementing 'best practices' wherever possible.

The early projects were naturally heavily based on American templates and practices, but this was found to be somewhat inappropriate for the UK and Europe, and many local adaptations were made to training, roll-out plans and project procedures. Time and effort expended by team members was at a premium, and the methodology was constantly being refined to remove excess burden and demand on the organization and yet remain effective. The process of instigating the Six Sigma quality initiative was continually adapted and refined as lessons were learnt and the business increased both the number and extent of quality projects.

Billing and invoices

In one of the very first projects to be undertaken, this team commenced work during the general launch stage of the Six Sigma quality initiative, so the visible success of the project was of para-mount importance. Success was defined in terms of completion and goal-delivery, adherence to the Six Sigma methodology, and promotion of the customer quality concept. The project lasted for eight months, as each stage in the methodology was new to all and had to be taken one step at a time, and extensive Six Sigma training was provided for everyone.

The core process identified for improvement was 'customer service', with billing and invoicing being part of the overall CTQ tree. It was deemed an appropriate project to start with because it had a direct impact on the customers' perception of quality, it would give a quick return to the business, and it included an anticipated area for improvement based on the expected error rate currently experienced with invoicing in general. Early customer survey indicated that only 25 per cent of customers rated the organization 'excellent' or 'very good' (top two points on a five-point scale) with regard to accuracy and completeness of invoices, with the target for such a rating being 80 per cent, leaving considerable room for improvement.

The principal CTQs were stated to be timeliness and accuracy. As was shown later in the project, the accuracy in the UK invoicing system was already better than that of the US parent company driving the project, due to a different computer system, a better level of software imple-mentation and a better level of existing quality assurance for data input. As the project progressed, the emphasis shifted, and the timeliness aspect was removed altogether, as it was not an immedi-ate issue and was certainly beyond the scope of such an early project.

Early measurement work identified that although invoicing amounted to only a quarter of all billing (direct debit accounting for almost three-quarters), almost half of all incoming payments arose by this means. The major customers still paid by invoice, with over 7000 payments collected on invoice each month. This highlighted the importance to the organization of invoicing, internal regard for which had diminished somewhat in favour of direct debit collections. At this time, additional work involving rejected direct debits was also removed from the scope of this project, and the project team concentrated solely on invoices.

Considerable debate raged over the issue of what exactly constituted a defect for the customer. As the project progressed, it was identified that for each invoice to be accurate, the customer would require a number of 'fields' on each invoice to be correct, and not just the payment amount. Various platforms issued different invoices, so the final agreed number of fields varied from 8 to as many as 12. Such fields included the payment amount, settlement date, customer name and address, VAT amount, and specific item billing details.

The process of invoice-production was mapped out, and it was decided to collect data that was already available, including the measurements for number and type of invoice. Such information was easily collected from the existing computer system. It was also noticed early on in the project that a number of customers would call the customer service department each month to make telephone enquiries about received invoices. No data was initially available on this, and it was necessary to introduce a manual logging system, completed by a sample of customer service staff for a period of two weeks. The total number of incoming calls was known from the telephone monitoring system, and this allowed data analysis to extrapolate the total proportion of all calls that related to invoices, and identify the reasons why each call had been made.

The final definition of a customer defect was stated to be either an error or omission in one of the eight fields on the invoice that were shown to matter to the customer. Defects were counted twice or more if any one customer-service call related to issues on two or more fields. The total number of opportunities for defect amounted to the number of invoices sent out multiplied by the number of fields per invoice. Errors in certain fields resulted in 'catastrophic failure' of the invoice, for example where the address was incorrect, and these were normally returned by the Post Office. Such defects from returned invoices, letters of complaint and enquiry were also added to the defect count, but only as one defect each.

After the measurement stage, it was shown that more than 1 in every 7 invoices sent out resulted in a call to customer services. In the case of a customer with 20 invoices over the life of a typical agreement, that customer would be unable to complete payment without resorting to further action on no less than three occasions. The impact of this was an excessive number of telephone calls received, dissatisfied customers, and a considerable delay in payment of due invoices, and was clearly quite unacceptable. The cost of poor quality was eventually calculated from the total impact of supporting these customer calls, processing returned invoices, generating manual reprints and computer record updates, loss of interest due to delay in payment, and from defaults from first payments (where most impact from invoice inaccuracy occurred). Added to this was a figure for the impact such poor quality would have on customer loyalty, and the return in profits gained as a result of a 1 per cent increment in the existing customer retention rate.

The total number of defects, including all calls, returned invoices and so on, amounted to about 1250 defects per month. The total number of opportunities amounted to 56 000 (8 opportunities per 7000 invoices), and from this the process performance value was calculated at 3.5 sigma. The cost of a defect was shown to be approximately £5, half of which was 'hard' costs, and the other half 'soft' costs. This amounted to an annual impact of £75 000 due to poor quality, and the initial project goal was to halve the number of defects and 'save' half of this cost.

Careful examination of the reasons for invoice issues in the UK business indicated that over 60 per cent of the problems were due to missing or incomplete data, rather than inaccurate data. Clearly, a number of items were expected by customers and were not currently being fully provided on the invoice. Solutions generated by the team focused on a redesign of the invoice to make it more 'customer-oriented'. A new field was added to the main details, and existing but unused fields were put to use by changing data collection processes, and by informing both staff and customers that such details could indeed be included. Benchmarking other industries showed that current best practice was to include extensive customer information on the reverse of the invoice, and the project team introduced a new design for the back of the standard company invoice.

A short manual trial of courtesy reply envelopes, aimed at speeding up payment and ensuring delivery to the correct postal address, did not show the anticipated levels of use for a cost-effective introduction, and this was not implemented as a solution. As part of the control mechanism, a totally new monitoring system was introduced for the customer call area, and new working practices allowed continuous logging of all types of enquiries. Not only did this allow for control and monitoring of this particular process, but it also opened up the way to easy measurements for future projects in other areas of customer service.

Not all of the solution-set was implemented in such a short period. A number of improvements to the invoice computer system were requested, but would obviously take several months to schedule and process. The impact was nevertheless dramatic, and control measurements indicated a monthly reduction in customer invoice-related calls from over 1000 to about 250 as a direct result of the changes made. In the short term, the difference was noticed in the customer service department, where in effect a resource equal to one member of staff had been freed up by the reduction in call rate, and normal working returned to this previously over-stretched department. In process terms, the final performance value was calculated at four sigma. Control was handed back to the champion, and the team was publicly rewarded for its success.

This particular project scenario is rather complex from the statistical and control point of view, and is probably not a good example with which to start. The project was completed more in the spirit of Six Sigma than in close adherence to the letter of it, but it was a considerable success for many reasons. A sympathetic champion, team leader and cross-functional team members, together with support from the newly formed quality department and senior management, ensured that all obstacles to progress were removed. The short-term impact was clear, and was demonstrably more effective and wide-ranging than had been expected or even hoped for. If nothing else, the project had worked. One difficulty was that defects were defined as discrete events, so no real continuous data could be collected, analysed and controlled. Binomial distributions are more appropriate to such processes than normal distributions, although there can be a very close approximation between them in such cases. For such an early project in a service industry quality initiative, strict adherence to Statistical Process Control was also very low on the list of priorities, and could easily wait until later projects.

Certain aspects of the invoice-production were generally highly company-focused, and very little customer focus and attention had ever been consciously applied to the process. Some project findings and recommendations were not applied in the short term, but were gradually added to a body of hard facts accumulating from later projects, until a critical mass of evidence propelled a major shift in tax-handling on invoices. The original mechanism had been put in place for purely internal financial reasons, and led to a considerable overhead in costs and poor customer relationships, but it had been difficult to assess the full impact since the effect was spread across the entire company.

Application processing cycle time

Another early project, this commenced during the learning stage of Six Sigma, and was the first quality initiative undertaken in a particular geographic location of the business. It was again important to deliver visible success for this location, in order to overcome any early scepticism, and also to continue to refine the process for running quality projects generally.

The process chosen was the credit approval section of initial applications from individuals and businesses. Here, the CTQ characteristic was definitely speed of response, and over half of customers had already indicated that the organization was neither 'excellent' nor 'very good' in this area. The process was easy both to define and to map, but the team expressed considerable uncertainty over the improvement target goal. No current measurements were being taken from this process, and it had been assumed that customers were generally happy with what was being delivered. The team was reluctant to set a goal until such time as the current performance had been quantified, and a believable improvement target set from this. The process was further complicated by the fact that it was split operationally depending on the type of customer involved, and two different CTQs had to be identified – one for personal customers, and one for commercial customers. The more onerous was for personal customers, and for simplicity only this CTQ will be discussed here. A watershed expectation of four hours was agreed as a starting point, and a small set of customers surveyed to gauge their reaction. On the understanding that it is not possible to please everyone, it was found that for a suggested process response of within four hours, 80 per cent of customers stated that they would be 'very satisfied', and a further 10 per cent 'satisfied'. However, for a process response over four hours, not one would be 'very satisfied', and only 60 per cent 'satisfied'. This confirmed that four hours was indeed a critical turning point, and to exceed customer expectation the final target was set at just two hours, half the customer expectation.

No measurements or control mechanisms were in place in this process at all, apart from counts and final volume of business. A manual data collection process was necessary, and again team reluctance to use sampling techniques eventually resulted in a complete census over a four-week period. The data collected included many anticipated factors, such as office location, size and type of agreement, incoming method (mail, fax or telephone), as well as elapsed time taken at many points during the entire process. Such a data collection plan was excessive, and resulted in considerable work, time and effort to collect, collate and analyse the data. However, pockets of resistance to the quality approach did exist at that time, and the refusal to complete data collection forms and the falsification of data for one reason or another were anticipated, met with and adjusted for in the final analysis.

The data collected was of excellent quality and quantity, and was based soundly on the continuous value for process time as well as several discrete characteristics of the process. Early descriptive analysis showed key behavioural patterns, such as the fact that three-quarters of incoming applications arrived by fax, and one-third arrived on a Monday morning. Early process map analysis also showed that considerable delays existed throughout, amounting to almost 90 per cent of the elapsed time taken. At this point, it became clear that there was substantial room for improvement, as well as a considerable need for it. The average process time was calculated at almost 180 minutes, or three hours. Figure 6.3 shows the plotted distribution shape, which is clearly heavily skewed and not a classical normal distribution at all. Over half of all applications were failing to be processed in the target time of two hours, giving a calculated process performance value of just 1.4 sigma. This clearly showed that for such a time-related process with a heavily skewed distribution, although the average time was not overly excessive, the total number of customers experiencing failures was. Extensive data analysis followed, using a range of inferential statistical techniques.

The data non-normality was corrected with a Box-Cox transform, and a *main effects plot* produced. Excessive distortion or skew in a frequency distribution is similar to looking through thick, coloured glass: it is difficult to see what is really happening and to gauge perspectives

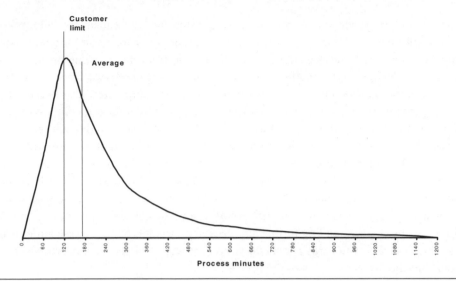

Figure 6.3 Process before improvement

correctly. The Box-Cox transform is simply an algorithm for working out how to reverse the distortion and return to the underlying normal distribution. Figure 6.4 shows how such a main effects plot can be used to easily identify principal root causes.

Here, the overall average is shown with the centre line, and the changes in value for a number of chosen factors are plotted in sections side by side. If any one factor changes dramatically, such as different offices or incoming methods, then such factors clearly have an effect on the outcome. Other factors, such as day of week or week number, may change little, and thus do not have the 'main effects' on the outcome. Using the data analysis findings and the observations from process

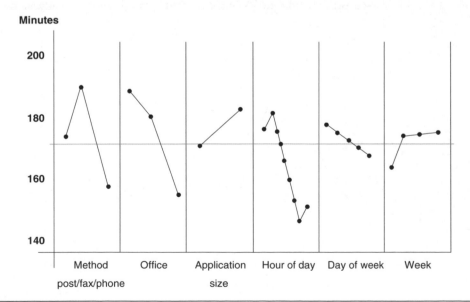

Figure 6.4 Main effects plot

mapping, the team was easily able to identify and quantify the root causes for failure to process applications within the two-hour target. Clearly, the fax machine contributed a quantifiable delay (of 25 minutes), as incoming faxes were not always removed from the machine promptly. Applications received by telephone, on the other hand, were taken by trained staff who could prompt for missing or inaccurate information, thus preventing processing delays later. Best practices peculiar to one branch, where staffing and procedures were slightly different, also highlighted several root causes for delay. Interestingly, it was found that processing speed was also directly related to application volume by hour and day of week, the reverse of what was found elsewhere and might have been assumed. When there is a greater number of applications per hour (early in the day), the processing time can often be shorter. This is due to batch techniques and bottlenecks, where paperwork is accumulated in a pile until a satisfactory quantity is available to be passed on to the next stage or person. Such behaviour can also result in a first-in, last-out reversal of paperwork at several points in the process, adding further unnecessary variation to the overall processing time. As this was the reverse to what was actually observed, it was clear that batch processing was not an issue, but that the overall capacity of the process was.

It was almost unnecessary to actively look for solutions, as the identified and quantified root causes directly implied what was necessary to improve the process. The data collected was sufficient for the team to suggest early quick-hit solutions to the sponsor, and action was taken on several counts immediately. By far the biggest impact came from implementing a new control process with key measurements introduced for the first time throughout the process, together with monitoring and control at the highest level. Solutions were all implemented rapidly, and control measurements revealed the dramatic impact. Average application processing time was reduced to under 70 minutes, and more importantly, the CTQ characteristic was now more normally distributed, with a process performance value better than three sigma. The process continued to be monitored using Statistical Process Control tools, and showed further improvements as the process changes took hold over the next few months. The final process sigma a year later was closer to four sigma, with an average process time of 45 minutes, and was remaining steady at that level (see Figure 6.5).

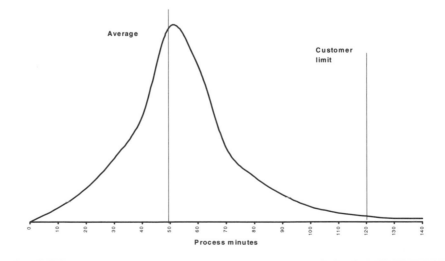

Figure 6.5 Process after improvement

The project was a *huge* success. For the customer, the number of applications failing to be processed in less than two hours had fallen from 55 per cent to less than 2 per cent. A survey of the top-ranking customers one year after the project finished clearly indicated that speed was indeed a critical issue for performance quality, and it had also shown that the delivery of outstanding performance had been noticed by customers, was highly welcome, and had resulted in an increase in business. Internal cynicism towards Six Sigma quality had been almost totally overcome, and the project became the base for a number of offshoot projects to follow, both locally and elsewhere.

Financial returns from the project were assessed in terms of cost savings, benefits from increased capacity, and improvements in customer loyalty and the revenue generated as a result. It is very difficult to save real money by simply reducing delays in a process, as in theory a delay costs nothing. In this case, one whole process step was removed, together with the necessary and very real processing costs. By far the greatest impact comes from the increased capacity to do business, which allowed for future growth without an increase in overheads. The final project savings were estimated at over £100 000 annually, far in excess of the quality improvement costs.

Process cycle time is a very popular CTQ characteristic to use, and easy to address by means of a project. This was one of three similar projects running at the same time, and a very productive one-day joint meeting of all three teams led to a new aspect of sharing and support between project teams. It was noticed that the 25-minute fax delay was universal world-wide!

The considerable success of the project to reduce delay prompted the question whether the initial target had been set low enough to start with. Other business teams working on similar processes had identified that their value-adding steps for this process only took about 15 minutes, so 15 minutes was taken as the very best possible target. Clearly, changing the customer target like this radically alters the calculated process sigma. In the short term, this project had to achieve a visible improvement, and it certainly did that. With a final process capability of about four sigma, further improvements would be unlikely without major technology and systems improvement. In benchmarking the industry generally, it had been noted that a close competitor guaranteed a similar process target of just one hour, which would also have been a good target for this team to adopt. However, it was perhaps too much of a stretch in the short term, and the performance of the competitor did not live up to local customer expectation. Indeed, some customers were not using the competitor's services simply because the process and the final result were so unreliable. The lesson to learn is that there are often several CTQs acting within one process, and it is important not to compromise other CTQs in the rush to improve just one. If the marketplace competition did change, then such targets would also have to be changed, immediately making the process perform at a lower sigma value, and it is advisable to set CTQ targets with a long life expectancy where possible.

Payment allocation

As a mid-term project, this team was set up during the improving stage of the quality initiative. By this time, project identification and roll-out was conducted according to a well-structured plan, and the rationale for undertaking projects had shifted from high-profile success and immediate return to a more general strategy of improvement and internal cultural change. The champion was very enthusiastic towards Six Sigma and quality in general, having promoted several earlier highly successful projects. However, the team leader chosen by the champion was generally sceptical of Six Sigma, and held a prominent and influential position within a major area of the company. The project was run as much to demonstrate and convince this person of the benefits of Six Sigma as it was to improve the process, which was a source of much internal frustration. Success was noted, in that the original (and self-confessed) doubter was self-implementing and promoting small improvement projects just six months after the close of this first project.

The project team ran for about four months, the entire process being accelerated by 'just in time' team training, good early project preparation, and an increasing level of awareness of Six Sigma within the company. Requests for project assistance and measurement data, as well as the implementation of process changes, were usually met with enthusiasm and a genuine desire to help.

The process itself was the recording, correct allocation and banking of incoming payment cheques from customers. The process had only recently been radically altered, and was therefore not an ideal candidate for such a project. It is best if processes are in a relatively stable state (statistically 'in control') before quality projects are undertaken, but the process was believed to be highly inefficient, was generating excessive workloads in certain areas, and a Six Sigma quality team was seen as the best way to deal with all the issues. The benefits from such a project would almost certainly be seen internally rather than by customers, and real cost savings were expected in terms of reducing staff involvement.

Early process mapping and measurement indicated that an average of approximately 250 cheques each day arrived at the post room, where they were directly logged and allocated to customer accounts on the computer system. Considerable variation in numbers was seen over a week, and during the month, with Monday mornings being the peak load time when the existing process was clearly failing to cope. The majority of the cheques were processed very rapidly and efficiently, and then sent to the finance department, whence they were taken to the bank just after lunchtime. Setting the customer target was difficult, as this process was not conspicuous to customers and was probably taken for granted. The team considered the impact of *not* allocating incoming cheques, and it was noted that this delayed banking and affected the customer service and credit control departments, which would be working with inaccurate customer accounts. A target of four hours (from 8.30 a.m.) was eventually accepted, as this allowed customers to assume posted cheques would credit their account on the same day as receipt, and would allow internal staff access to correct account information after midday. As cheques were banked shortly after lunch, such a target also benefited the company through the fastest possible application of credit to the company account. It had already been shown from an earlier project that non-payment of the average invoice amounted to a loss of interest equivalent to 22 pence each day, and speeding the entire process up by just one day amounted to an annual benefit of £15 000 from this point alone.

Measurements concentrated on 'fact-finding' to quantify the current position, and to assist in identifying the root causes for failure in allocating cheque payments correctly within the four-hour limit. Measurements collected were principally discrete data rather than continuous data, and much difficulty was experienced, both in collection and analysis. However, this did not ultimately detract from the overall success of the project. It was found that 80 per cent of all cheques were allocated normally, taking about four hours' work in total each day from all the many people involved. However, in sharp contrast, the other 20 per cent of cheques were the exceptions, and led to considerable additional work. Up to six further people were involved with each cheque not immediately allocated, and estimates for the total work required ranged from 20 to 30 person-hours per day. Without deploying one-way mirrors, stopwatches and hidden cameras, it was impossible to ascertain exactly how much time was being spent on the exceptions, but conservative estimates showed that the aggregated equivalent of two full-time staff could possibly be released across several departments. Because the work involved so many people, and usually took only five or ten minutes now and then, both measuring and ensuring that such savings were converted from figures to reality were very difficult indeed. Human judgement is highly subjective, and people tend to play down the amount of time they spend on trivia and inflate the time they spend more fruitfully. Further, relieving someone of a daily ten-minute chore does not necessarily mean that such time will be saved and used productively elsewhere. There is, however, a cumulative effect upon staff who are required to perform tasks knowing that there is little benefit and gain, and all involved were highly enthusiastic, and indeed hopeful, that something was about to be done about this poorly performing and tedious process.

The initial situation showed that about 10 per cent of cheques were unallocated within the CTQ limit, setting the process performance at about 2.8 sigma. It was also possible to show that such cheques then spent an average of four days being resolved, during which time further complications arose if the customer contacted the company (or vice versa) for any reason, which was often the case.

The team aimed to reduce the number of exceptions to about a tenth of their current number, and to radically improve the process of dealing with these unallocated cheques. Most implemented solutions concentrated on improving the workflow balance and ensuring ownership of the problem and the authority to take action. Extra staff were allocated at peak times, and excess staff removed from any unnecessary steps within the process. Employees that were more senior were deployed at the critical points in the process, and a new control and reporting process was put in place to ensure problems were dealt with swiftly.

Several major changes to the invoicing system were requested, as it was observed that a quarter of all problems resulted from issues 'up-stream' of this process. Such implementation was again not possible in the short time scale, but was added to other pending requests for future action. The final improvement observed showed that less than 2 per cent of cheques remained unallocated by the deadline, giving a process performance of about 3.8 sigma. A very positive additional benefit was that the existing backlog of cheques awaiting investigation was entirely cleared once and for all. Much was learnt from this project, and clearly the benefits were much more wide-ranging than just immediate customer satisfaction. The expressed view was that finally the company had an effective method by which poorly performing processes could be improved and resultant gains effectively monitored. In this particular case, the original process was one that had already been radically changed and redesigned, and yet still performed very badly. The remaining question was how to introduce new processes with the inherent capability of a better performance right from the start.

SUMMARY

- Implementing Six Sigma is about initiating a cultural change in the way an organization thinks about itself and its environment, and putting in place the necessary enablers and structures for this to happen. Launching such a TQM initiative requires a mission, objectives, a strategic plan, and tools and techniques.
- To underpin any TQM strategy, an organization must have effective and sufficient resources, and a willingness and adeptness in the areas of commitment, planning, training, communication and change-management.

- Over time, any Six Sigma strategy is likely to pass through several stages, which generally include:
  1 preparation, including cultural and change initiatives, as well as early benchmarking and customer assessment;
  2 launching and promoting Six Sigma within the organization;
  3 learning the Six Sigma methodology and its application by means of early projects;
  4 improving and locally refining the methodology and quality project roll-out;
  5 mastering Six Sigma as an ongoing journey.

- Quality teams, using a simple but rigorous step-by-step methodology, are perhaps the best way to implement TQM process improvement, certainly during the early stages of the quality initiative. One such Six Sigma methodology of choice is based on the stages of:
  1 pre-work, including project identification and justification;
  2 formal definition of the project;
  3 measurement of CTQ characteristics and key factors;
  4 analysis of data and process;
  5 improvement of the process;
  6 control, evaluation and process handover.

- Champions of quality are essential for the successful implementation of process improvements and quality teams. Champions need to demonstrate visible commitment to Six Sigma by their actions. To this end, they need to hold a vision of customer-driven quality, to actively want to improve and change, and must measure processes, not people. They should be leading rather than commanding, enhance communication, and empower employees to act.

- Change-management and change culture also plays a very important part in implementing project solutions. For any change to be successful, the acceptance of change is as important as the change itself. To ensure maximum acceptance of change, there must be a visible reason for it, the change process must be well facilitated, and the motivation for change must be lasting.

- A typical Six Sigma initiative will require involvement from several tiers of staff. Visible lead and commitment comes from the very top via champions. A few highly skilled individuals provide wide-ranging expertise and coaching support, with further full-time staff directly supporting and running the quality projects and teams. Part-time staff will lead a team as required, and general engagement is maintained by involving many employees from the organization as cross-functional team members.

- Quality assurance and management tools such as ISO 9000 can play a number of useful roles within an overall TQM strategy. Early quality assurance work with processes will benefit and accelerate Six Sigma project work, and assurance and process standardization assist immensely with ongoing control. However, in the long term, quality assurance and management control should be regarded as assisting rather than directing TQM initiatives.

CHAPTER SEVEN

Looking to the Future

Six Sigma involves much more than simply running a few quality teams to improve poor performance in existing processes. Long-term successes will depend upon the organization's ability to align to customer processes, to ensure consistency and control without regimentation, and to continually adapt to the changing environment. As Six Sigma quality improvement is itself inevitably carried out through a process, this too must evolve and adapt to the changing needs of the organization.

TQM is about change within an organization and its processes, and it may be tempting to say that when 'sufficient' change has taken place, the impetus and drive can decline and take a back seat. In the application of Six Sigma quality, process change must be driven forward constantly, as any change in customer requirements will always degrade current process performance, and the cycle of improvement will begin again. Incremental improvements move process performance forwards, but with a decreasing return on the increasing investment required, it eventually becomes necessary to radically alter inherent process capability through exponential change and redesign.

PROCESS-ORIENTED ORGANIZATIONS

It is clear that for any organization to be effectively customer-centric and ever-responsive to changing customer needs, core processes must always take precedence. In many businesses, events such as 'customer refunds' or 'product shipping' may cross many departments and business functions, and can take weeks to complete. In contrast, customer expectations for such processes may amount to little more than hours or days, and ensuring both delivery and consistency of such performance demands streamlined processes.

The vision that emerges from a successful Six Sigma initiative is that of a company where the customer comes first, and where key processes are driven for the customer and measured against customer-set targets and specifications. Such customer-centric processes can only run effectively if a new type of manager captains them: one who instinctively champions the customer and responds directly to the needs of the process. TQM inevitably calls for a new attitude from management, but rarely proposes any substance to demonstrate how this can apply in everyday operation. Process-ownership is one practical embodiment of such a radical managerial change, plus a decisive vision for the future of organizations driven firmly by customer quality.

In old-style companies, the shipping department may be positioned at the end of the production line process. The production line dominates, and is both customer and supplier to the shipping process. Realistically, shipping exists merely to take away production at the end of the day, and the true external customer has become subservient to production. However, from the external customer viewpoint, shipping may be the key process that delivers the goods after ordering. For the customer, shipping should actually drive the process of production, and fully customer-centric management can only occur if this subtle change in structure is implemented.

TQM initiatives may be highly successful in the short term, and can motivate far-reaching cultural change and process improvement. For a period, shipping and production may work well together, meeting each other's needs, and meeting the targets and goals set by the external customer. However, in time the customer targets will undoubtedly change and become more demanding. If, for example, a competitor were to shift from a position of delivery three days after ordering to offering customer-specified and named-day delivery, the existing processes of shipping and production are unlikely to cope with such a change. If timely delivery is a major CTQ characteristic for the external customer, then the competitor will soon take the dominant market position, and process change must start all over again. Management tends to exist to protect the resource and functionality of each unit in an organization, and it would not generally be possible for the shipping manager to rapidly instigate the necessary changes in the production process to meet a new customer delivery specification. Rather, the organization would have to drive change in production, and then realign shipping to suit, all of which is both difficult and time-consuming.

A radical difference occurs if shipping is treated as a core customer process, and production becomes a subservient function of the organization. Now shipping is managed as the dominant process, aligned and responsive to external customer needs. A change in the environment, caused by competitive markets, allows the shipping process-owner to adjust the shipping processes internally, and to pass internal requirements for inputs (the goods to be shipped) back down to production, which is now firmly the supplier to shipping. Production, in its turn, responds to the changing needs of the customer (shipping), and adjusts internal processes accordingly.

Such responsiveness only occurs when each process becomes master of its own destiny, and the process-owner has all the resources and functionality needed within the sphere of control. Ideally, shipping would have the necessary dedicated business functionality covering such matters as information technology, finance, human resources, and so on. The organization will perhaps begin to model the pattern of a well-constructed computer program, where the ultimate functionality seen by the end user is driven by a very light framework dictating the overall performance and operation, and is supported by a series of primitive functions which actually carry out the work. Each user-task required by the program is completed by a number of functions, which will not themselves have to change if new user-tasks are required. All that needs to be done is to change the way in which the primitive functions operate, perhaps adding new functions or changing the parameters governing the performance of each function.

For organizations that shift to a customer-centric process operation, supported by business functionality, two benefits will be seen. Firstly, changes in external customer requirements can be cascaded rapidly and effectively within the organization, and still allow each unit the freedom to adjust and adapt quickly as required. Secondly, the organization as a whole becomes very much more responsive to the external and critical factors that directly influence overall success.

If process-management is the way forward to making an organization more responsive and adaptable to change, then process-ownership is the responsibility that comes with this change. The process-owner of tomorrow has a new challenge to meet, and a new set of tools to work with. Wherever possible, Statistical Process Control should be used to gauge whether each process is running within its capabilities and without excessive and unnatural variation. Customer surveys and opinions should be continuously monitored and responded to, and each process should be designed to perform to tightly controlled limits set by the customer.

Control charts have been used extensively within Statistical Process Control in manufacturing, and there is no reason why they cannot be used in service-related processes. Once a monitoring system has been put in place, producing control charts becomes a routine task, and is often easy to automate. The issue here is that such charts need to be up to date, available, and very much in use at all times. Control charts are simply indicators of inherent performance, and it is essential that appropriate action is taken in response. Often, processes are poorly controlled, or even worse, management responds violently to every natural vacillation in output. Naturally occurring variation dictates that outcomes and measures will normally differ from hour to hour or month to month within a given range, and this should be expected. This type of variation requires a long-term strategy to identify, understand and reduce it through ongoing process management and improvement. This takes time and effort, much as quality improvement teams do, and such quality teams are an excellent means of gradually reducing such natural variation. Special causes of variation, inherently unnatural in origin, require quite different and immediate action. Critical to such a response is the early collection of data to gain advance warning of changes, the rapid location of the cause, and appropriate management action. As special causes of variation are not due to the process itself, it is a mistake to adjust the process in any way in response. Often, the typical reaction to natural variation is to do nothing to the process, and for special-cause variation, the reaction is to adjust and tinker with the process – quite the opposite to what should actually happen. Such inappropriate action only serves to drive the process into increasingly violent oscillation, and often makes matters worse.

For example, the sales figures for a business each month will vary even for a process that is well managed and statistically 'in control'. Such variation arises from natural causes such as the random number of customers during each period, the changing seasonal weather, sales effectiveness, consumer demand and other such factors. To reward good sales figures for any one month, and hence punish bad figures, is to act without due rational cause. Natural variation in sales should be reduced over time as a management-led task to gradually improve the sales process, perhaps by using quality teams. In contrast, unnatural variation can be due to such factors as a new low-price competitor opening a shop across the road, leading to an overall decline in sales. In this instance, there is good reason to act, identify the cause and contain the damage. The sales process itself should not be changed, but rather the root cause of the special-cause variation should be dealt with, perhaps by lowering prices.

The difficulty all process-owners need to overcome is the erroneous tendency to attempt to manipulate naturally varying outcomes, and yet ignore the variation due to exceptions that require rapid and effective response.

FROM TWO TO FOUR SIGMA

As most processes generally seem to level out at a performance of between two and three sigma, it is never particularly difficult to make impressive gains from the very start of a new quality initiative. Each application of a quality project can easily lead to a tenfold defect reduction, with corresponding cost savings, and the gains by far outweigh the overheads in staff training and implemented changes.

This is the best time to fully engage the entire company by running many cross-functional teams. The problem is how to first release the resources that such a widespread engagement will undoubtedly require. In many organizations, there may not be the necessary slack and redundancy to provide the temporary effort and input of time required. The driving force for early projects must be both to act as a catalyst for the introduction of quality and change, and to release resources from processes to aid the quality initiative. If the long-term agenda is to reduce overall staffing levels, then this will clearly detract from the upbeat message required for change, and it is likely to apply a stigma to the quality initiative that will at best be very hard to shift. Far better if the organization aims to drive change and process improvement head-on for increased revenue, resulting from process savings and increased efficiency, and also from higher customer satisfaction leading to increased sales. This alone is a very positive message, and can rapidly build a level of enthusiasm within the organization that becomes self-sustaining. It is important to make the results from quality projects highly public, and to feed some of the gains made back into extending and deepening the quality effort. For example, if internal gains made go directly towards the quality effort elsewhere, and external gains go towards the bottom-line profit, then a good balance for payoff can be achieved. The first quality projects therefore need to attempt to provide both internal and external gains.

Early projects need to be supported by enthusiastic staff, and to have a clear route to success. Selecting projects to begin the initiative can be very difficult, as there is no single process that can guarantee any particular result from process improvement. Customer-focused processes from the middle core and service end of the organization can offer some of the easiest gains, and benefit well from being addressed by cross-functional quality teams. Financial processes such as invoicing, billing and accounting generally tend to operate at a higher level of performance, and also tend to be the least amenable to rapid change. Anything that relies heavily on information technology and the company computer system is best avoided in the first instance. Sales processes likewise pose initial difficulties (in terms of running teams and making changes, not the processes themselves), and benefit from early exclusion until such time as the Six Sigma improvement process is better understood and generally accepted. Any process directly touching the customer will return good results in increased loyalty, but immediate financial gains and savings are better made from more internally oriented improvements. Similarly, time-related processes can be improved dramatically by removing delay and rework, but eliminating delay will not in itself lead immediately to an increase in bottom-line profits. Some of the best early work can be found in departments that are over-stretched and under-resourced. It may be difficult to spare time and resources from the department itself, but by bringing in the first quality teams predominantly staffed from other departments, and using only one or two key employees from the process in question, fresh approaches and ideas can rapidly be brought to bear. Process mapping will certainly identify areas for immediate improvement, and with care an early project team may be able to implement several quick-hit solutions to free resources within the first two or three months of the project. The end impact of such a team will certainly be a reduction in workload for the department, and nothing acts better to promote Six Sigma quality than such a direct internal fillip.

Once the introduction of Six Sigma is well under way, from the cultural change point of view it is better to spread projects around, and to direct quality improvement efforts to all parts of the business. For maximum customer impact, projects need to be concentrated on just a few CTQs and core processes, but it is the weakest link that makes the customer–supplier chain break, and an alternative approach of bringing all processes up to the same standard has many benefits. Six Sigma is a very visible measurement approach to TQM, and soon everyone in the organization will be interested in ensuring that they are not left behind with the lowest process performance. Differences of more than one sigma-value in any process will highlight the difference, both internally and externally, and a balance should be restored as soon as is practicable. For example, all processes could work towards a four sigma target initially, and some processes may be already performing at that level. Four sigma in all processes implies a tenfold to one hundredfold gain or better on the unimproved situation, and will present an excellent public image, as well as eliminating many defects. No single project can return the perfect mix of results, and only by covering all possible areas and projects will the overall impact be closer to that ultimately required.

A level playing field of commonality also underpins the concept that TQM and Six Sigma apply to every employee, and success hinges upon imparting new skills, culture and vision to each employee in the organization. No one should be missed out, and all should be given the opportunity to become involved in one way or another. Even if the only direct involvement with Six Sigma takes the form of assisting with a project running within the department, no member of staff will be able to avoid feeling the impact from quality.

Beyond four sigma, many factors begin to influence the effectiveness of the perhaps too simplistic approach of quality teams. A natural ceiling for process improvement will be met, partly because of diminishing returns from defect-reduction. Establishing the cost benefits according to defects alone implies that improvement from 1 per cent failure to 0.1 per cent will not justify the time and effort from six employees for one day a week over six months. Further, changes to processes will be limited by the capacity of the existing process to perform at this level. If a Six Sigma initiative is taken seriously, the targets set by sound customer analysis will advance performance needs far beyond the original terms of operation. For example, if the customer currently receives an evening meal from room service in one hour, but wants it within 15 minutes, the gap in performance must be closed. Removing delays and wasted effort from the delivery process may reduce the time taken to 30 minutes. However, if all the essential steps by which the process must operate currently take 20 minutes in all, the gap cannot be closed by process improvement alone. New technology and process redesign are necessary to move beyond four sigma.

BEYOND FOUR SIGMA

To go beyond a process performance equivalent to four sigma is to venture into an area of excellence way beyond the normal. It therefore requires a combination of abnormal effort, cunning and commitment to achieve such a performance, which effort alone is unlikely to deliver. At issue are the inherent capabilities of the process, and the effectiveness of the cyclic application of team-led quality improvement.

There can be no doubt that six sigma performance is always achievable, generally by throwing money at the problem. In the supply of domestic electricity, perhaps just two critical factors – the consistency of availability, and the supplied voltage – govern the quality. Most supply companies talk about 99 or 99.9 per cent supply availability, whereas Six Sigma implies a measure of parts per million, and at a six sigma performance, domestic supply would fail completely for just 90 seconds each year. This is indeed possible, with a robust national grid, reliable generators and dual systems that can switch to alternative supplies automatically. Such an advanced level of performance relies on the design of the supply system as much as it does on the controlled operation of the component parts, but does so at the expense of over-engineering. The lean organization of today requires both capability in performance and efficiency in operation, and this has to be designed into the process from the start.

Figure 7.1 shows the performance of two processes, A and B, which might be the time taken to fit a replacement exhaust system for a motor car. The upper customer limit here has been set at 60 minutes, and the lower limit, by default, at zero, although customers would usually be highly suspicious of any organization which took less than about 15 minutes to carry out such work. Since in such a situation it is impossible in practice to have values below zero, the lower limit can

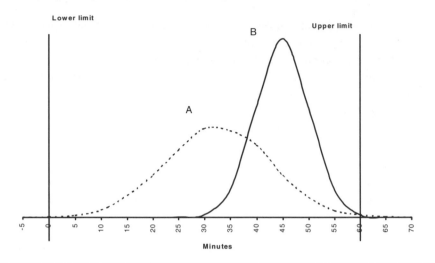

Figure 7.1 Process capability design

be ignored in favour of just the one upper limit. Both processes show neat normal distributions (perhaps too neat), and process A has an average of about 30 minutes and a large standard deviation of about 10 minutes. Process B, on the other hand, has an average of about 45 minutes, with a much smaller standard deviation of just 5 minutes. Both processes have three standard deviations between the mean and the upper customer limit. In pure metric terms, both processes therefore have almost an identical performance, which is about four-and-a-half sigma (allowing for the 1.5 sigma shift), and it would therefore seem that both processes perform identically for the customer.

From a customer point of view, process B may in fact be a better performer, in that the organization could guarantee to change the exhaust in under an hour, and perhaps more importantly, can deliver between 40 and 50 minutes for almost all customers. If customers were asked to come back in 55 minutes, few would have to wait, and those that did would wait only a few minutes. There is much less variation in the outcome compared to process A, where many customers asked to come back after 30 minutes may have a long wait – almost a further 30 minutes in all.

From the viewpoint of process improvement, these two processes pose totally different challenges and opportunities. It is unlikely to be possible to speed up process A, whereas process B has considerable leeway for reducing the average and shifting the whole curve to the left. If the end goal is six sigma process performance, then the owner of process B will have a tough job reducing variation further and making the curve thinner, whereas process A has much more room for manoeuvre.

From the viewpoint of the organization, process A is a better bet, as it would be possible to delay early completion of the work and provide a more consistent finish time, provided there is the capacity to hold completed vehicles awaiting collection. Shape A could be turned into shape B, with care. However, if the customer limit changed from 60 to 45 minutes, the customer performance of process B would be severely affected. No longer is a simplistic process improvement possible, and now careful design and consideration must be applied.

Figure 7.2 shows two possible scenarios from advanced research into customer expectations. The two shapes outline completely differing acceptable performances, and indicate clearly how a simplistic satisfied/not satisfied customer limit can hide the true picture. Target T_1 is very fast

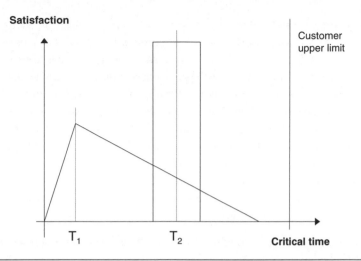

Figure 7.2 Process capability targets

compared with T_2, but shows more tolerance to variation. Target T_2 allows more time for the process, but has a very sharp cut-off either side. Only very careful questioning, research and even pilot trials would provide this information, but once obtained, the process could be tailored precisely to meet the customer need.

As drawn, the suggested targets T_1 and T_2 and the outcomes from processes A and B match as pairs reasonably well. For the example of changing an exhaust system, target T_2 and process B are more likely to match real life, and the challenge for the organization is to make the process meet the given target. This is no longer a case of speeding up the processes, but of reducing variation and strictly controlling the outcome. Considerable variation exists in the type of vehicle and exhaust system, the component parts to be replaced, the demand from minute to minute, and the available resources in terms of parts and staff. No longer is it appropriate to rely on quality circles or process improvement teams. No longer can output performance rely solely on control and operational assurance. Now is the time to bring in experts to design a process with the inherent capability to deliver time after time exactly to the customer requirements.

DESIGNING NEW PROCESSES

Past experiences with designing and launching new products or services show that a proportion fail to deliver to expectation, or simply fail altogether. Reasons for this are numerous, but include inadequate market analysis, problems with the product itself, technical or production issues, and a failure to fully comprehend costs and competitive strengths. Typically, a very large proportion of all effort is expended after the launch, and not before, which reduces successful impact and payoff returns overall. Few organizations seem to be able to get a new product or service right first time, and those that aspire to Six Sigma must deliver exceptional performance from the start.

Any methodology that aims to design for six sigma performance needs to address internal issues as well as external customer requirements. Design is not the end goal in itself, and any methodology for six sigma design must fit within a larger plan for the introduction of new products and services. If process improvement is an incremental change, then design is an exponential change, and should ideally deliver a process operating at four sigma or better, with the capability to improve to six sigma performance in perhaps just two improvement loops using a quality team. Achieving such a goal requires a new methodology, as small improvements generally work best by springing from what already exists, whereas totally new processes do not have any background or history to work from. Six Sigma is relatively new and still advancing, and such Six Sigma design methodologies are still evolving, even at the beginning of the new century. Many organizations are actively attempting to rationalize theory and empirical experience from Six Sigma design into a concise and workable whole. Once such a design tool has evolved to a working state within an organization, it can also be used by process-owners to drive rapid change in situations where poor inherent capabilities limit current or future process improvement.

In designing a new process or product, either for service or manufacturing, the total requirement from the process or product must be:

- the ability to produce or deliver to specification, including costs and ongoing control;
- robustness and resilience in terms of error, failure and exception;
- a good match to customer expectation and satisfaction.

As well as attempting to deliver on the above points, it is as well to realize that other enigmas lurk within the mastery of Six Sigma, in that early quality initiatives can, if driven to their logical conclusions, stifle and restrict processes even more than before they were introduced. If the aim is to remove all traces of variation and slack from a process, then doing so by rigid control of staff is a serious mistake. It must be clear that control is applied to processes and variation, which are the enemy, *not* the employees. Ultimately, processes need to be designed not only for customer performance, but also for controllability and ease of operation. Such designer processes will offer everything required by the customer, and the organization, and yet allow freedom and necessary expression for all employees involved. Customer call centres, for example, are still increasing in popularity as an end-goal for efficiency in dealing with the symptoms of customer-related problems. Recent research is beginning to unearth the inevitable truth – that such call centre processes are rarely designed with either customer or employee in mind. Customers are showing the early signs of dislike of badly run call centres, and employees are showing signs of overload and fatigue from the purely mind-numbing tasks involved. How much better to adopt a Six Sigma philosophy and remove the need for the customer to call in the first place!

In the early days of electronics, transistor circuit designers planned the operating performance of each circuit around the design specifications of the transistors involved. Any such component that was out of specification would make the circuit fail, and manufacturers scrapped defective transistors. Sir Clive Sinclair commenced his entrepreneurial career by buying a batch of discarded transistors, and designing several useful circuits wherein the performance was not reliant in any way upon the central transistor. In these designs, cheap and cheerful transistors could be used to great effect, and so it must be with the design of service and manufacturing processes. One of the greatest insights into the long-term application of Six Sigma is the realization that every aspect of the performance of a process should be designed. It is this that makes possible a move from trying to fit square pegs into round holes to a position where the size and shape of the hole does not matter. As far as possible, the behaviour of the entire process should be independent of the internal characteristics of the constituent parts and resources.

Pure design is a highly creative activity, and in some instances operates without restraint or goal. However, ask any design consultant how they work, and the answer will be that design starts from a set of guidelines or restraints, within which the design process must operate freely. The secret in designing for six sigma performance is to start with the customer and build up a set of parameters and constraints for the design process to operate within. Only by ensuring that the design stage commences with, and thus embodies, a well-defined customer specification can the six sigma capability of the final process be guaranteed. Typical design commences with a brief from the organization or process-owner, and many organizations have completely ignored the customer and employee, at their peril.

All design has the aim of finding the best possible solution within the given parameters. Ensuring that the final solution obtained is indeed the best requires a deep understanding of all the judgement criteria, and that every influencing aspect has been considered. The Japanese quality movement and manufacturing industry of today realize the vital importance of covering every aspect in design, as well as sound customer analysis. To this end, a number of very powerful tools have evolved to assist with the steps required to go from customer needs to design para-meters. Add to this a number of piloting, testing and verification tools, together with excellent project management, budgeting and control, and the result is a method for designing for inherent six sigma capability and performance.

The stages involved can be outlined as follows:

1 conception and business planning of a solution;
2 prototyping and advanced development;
3 project-definition and design-refinement;
4 conducting customer analysis to define service or product parameters;
5 conceptualizing, refining and selecting solution features to meet these parameters;
6 drawing up a full design, covering all aspects of the final solution;
7 piloting and testing, refining and implementing the solution;
8 exercising control, including ongoing cyclic process improvement.

For example, in designing a new restaurant that will deliver a product and service at better than four sigma performance from the day of opening, the stages would start with the conception of the restaurant theme, size, location and type. Then might follow the designing and trialing of a few menus and kitchen equipment, particularly if the concept was radical in nature. After that, the design project could begin in earnest with a full definition of the project, and customer needs analysis of service delivery and the food product. The solution concept would then be developed further to include a possible mix of features, such as number of tables, layout and service techni-ques and food served, which together would best satisfy all of the customer needs. Such needs would also include the internal customers, such as staff and management, as well as shareholders. The parameters for all proposed features would then be rigorously defined to ensure that when designed, if the whole solution met the design criteria, it would also meet the customer require-ments at a high-sigma performance. Given these requirements, which would list such things as number of items on the menu, time to order and time to deliver food to table, quantity of food and type of service, the entire design solution could then proceed to a fully detailed blueprint. At this stage, the blueprint, in theory at least, would satisfy all the criteria, and hence all the customer requirements. The next step would be to pilot the plan and verify that it would indeed work, followed by any necessary refinement, and then full implementation. The final step is to move into the typical control stage, which might require further team-based quality improvement, as has already been discussed.

The use of quality teams for such design is now again cost-effective, as a new solution implies increased efficiency, lower costs, additional revenue from the new product or service, as well as a better capability, both now and in the near future. All the costs involved can be offset against the benefits, and this may be the only practical way in which organizations can move beyond the four sigma performance barrier. Such total design work also deals with the issue of multiple CTQ characteristics and possible conflicts between them, which is generally ignored in simple process improvements. New tools used in such design will include *Quality Function Deployment* (QFD), which assists with the difficult task of providing a bridge between customer needs and firm requirement specifications. QFD also allows conflict between multiple needs to be assessed, but it does require considerable work. Full application of these tools can easily identify several hundred characteristics that affect customer perception of quality, and designing a new process may require analysis and consideration of all of these in their totality.

In practice, a more hybrid team would be used for such design work, combining quality skills such as customer analysis with technical design support. In advanced design cases, it may well be more suitable to change teams part way through, and to use a quality team from the sharp end of the business to cover up to stage five in the list above. This at least ensures that all the criteria handed to the team responsible for the actual design are soundly based on customer and business needs, and will ensure that successful design leads to excellent process performance. Another point to note is that design can also become cyclic in an organization, in that products or services are improved and launched in stages. Here, the long-term view is essential to ensure future-proof design that provides a path for continuous development and marketing, as well as outstanding long-term quality performance.

USE OF TECHNOLOGY

In the commercial world today, new technology is often the leading force for process change and product advancement, but it is a double-edged sword that can both hamper and assist process improvements. In the late 1990s, the rise in the use of the Internet and the World Wide Web has been astounding, and has left many organizations keen to get involved and find new ways of using the technology. Here, technology that is new (to commerce, in any case) has provided a solution before there is a need for it, and the rush to find a need often results in an inappropriate use of the solution. Technology used poorly and for the wrong reasons always delivers poor customer performance. Success can only be assured if change is *led* by the business, based on customer needs and *assisted* by new technology, not the other way round. Since technology is often highly complex, the necessary experts are usually quite far removed from both business and customer. It sometimes appears that the joy of having a new toy to play with excludes practical sense and reason, and technology becomes something to use for its own sake. Video recorders are a classic case, where technocrats rather than customers dictated the person–machine interface, the end result being that ordinary people find it difficult to use such devices. Just because shopping on the Internet is possible, or even fun, does not mean that it intrinsically solves customer needs, and neither does it imply better quality or a better process in any way. Early experiences show that in many cases such e-commerce systems make more work for the supplier, are difficult for the consumer, and are highly prone to error. Where the final product or service is actually worse than when not using the new technology, only the minority of die-hard technocrats will use the option, further enhancing the overall impression that it is not for the average consumer.

The application of sensible and appropriate technology is vital for any organization today, and without doubt, this is the only way to progress any long-term quality initiative. To err is human, and manual production and quality control will always deliver a small proportion of failure. Progressing beyond a 99 per cent success rate requires automatic processes, generally using technology to remove the human root of failure. Only automation can deliver speed and repeated success with small and well-controlled ongoing variation, and such automation can often assist with further process measurement and control. The introduction of bar-coding and scanning systems has revolutionized grocery shopping, in terms of both accuracy and speed at the checkout. There are also real benefits for the organization in terms of what is now possible with bar-codes and scanning, and 'smart card' technology of the near future will extend the possibilities even further. Advances in technology generally bring opportunities for smarter ways to perform tasks and processes, and ways to remove error and variation.

Getting the very best from technology demands breaking new ground in old, stale processes limited in what can realistically be achieved. By re-inventing a process in totally new directions, giant leaps forward with customer service and efficient delivery become possible. Rather than trying to squeeze Internet shopping into grocery retailing, a far better approach is to go back to the basics involved, and to discover the vital customer needs of the shopping process. Process redesign, armed with the fresh potential new technology brings, allows the suggestion of new features that can solve customer needs more effectively. By using a rigorous approach with Six Sigma quality in mind, it is also possible to redesign a process with new technology to deliver at a much higher level of quality. As has already been discussed, grocery shopping is all about identifying, collecting, purchasing and transporting necessary items. All of this has a number of CTQ characteristics which measure how well any solution matches the customer needs, and the modern supermarket clearly meets a set of these better than the corner shop can, or else supermarket shopping would not dominate the UK retail grocery trade as it does. Limitations in supermarket shopping stem from the *physical* necessity to locate, collect and then pay for goods, and the only way of driving performance forward is to completely redesign the process, avoiding the physical necessities by using new technology. Internet shopping, as a new technology, offers the opportunity to alter radically what is possible in identifying, collecting and delivering goods, and it can also remove the need to queue for a checkout altogether.

In the year 2000, the Tesco supermarket chain is leading the way in introducing and expanding the range of Internet grocery shopping facilities in the UK. However, a closer look at how this is being done shows that it is simply an application of new technology to a very old process. Rather than going back to the basic customer needs involved and redesigning the process from scratch, major investment is being made in a process that effectively returns to the old ways of 'we serve you'. In contrast, petrol stations over the past thirty years have used technology to radically change the way in which the purchase process operates, both to reduce costs and increase quality performance in terms of speed and ease of use. It is now possible to drive into a petrol station, swipe a credit card at the pump, fill up, and go. Not only does this reduce internal operating costs and increase the capacity for business throughput, it also drastically improves the speed and ease-of-use quality characteristics for the consumer. For Internet shopping to challenge the *status quo* successfully, it must be more effective and efficient to run, and hence reduce operating costs, and must deliver a better-quality performance across all or most customer CTQs. This means that it must be faster, more accurate, easier, less effort, and cheaper. Whatever the solution is that will ultimately replace supermarket grocery shopping as we knew it in the 1990s, it must ensure that every item required is purchased, it should remove the need to physically locate and collect goods, it should remove the checkout, and it should provide transport to home. Moreover, above all of this, the process must perform better than before, with less variation and a higher level of quality.

If the solution adopted is to arrange for customers to e-mail their orders to stores, where staff carry out the identification, location and collection of the goods, then accuracy in item-selection will be lower than the customer can achieve, and efficiency will certainly not improve. The costs involved are likely to be passed on to the consumer, and there will remain a tension between the partial benefits and added value of the new service compared to the old. Enterprising grocery businesses continue to operate from the back of a small van, removing the need to visit a shop and transport goods home, and local grocery shops have been taking orders over the telephone and sending out a delivery person on a bike for years. Where, then, is the advantage in cost-efficiency or better service offered by an e-commerce supermarket chain? In the UK, the Safeway supermarket chain adopted an alternative solution several years ago, using the more radical technology and approach of giving customers access to individual scanners. Here, by means of self-scanning when selecting items off the shelves, the checkout process has almost been eliminated. Without the need to unload, scan and reload, the CTQs for the checkout process have been dramatically improved, and cost savings in reduced checkout staff and checkout machinery can offset the new technology. Quite clearly, in this instance the appropriate technology is a powerful enabler for the new process of self-scanning, and there must be considerable doubts as to what new benefits Internet supermarket shopping will actually bring in the short term.

As well as its questionable impact on CTQs, new technology also brings new problems with control and consistency. Whenever a process is radically altered, the measurement and control mechanisms must be updated to match. When all things are considered, it is perhaps *consistency* of performance that is most required by the customer, and nothing infuriates more than processes failing because of 'bad' technology. When new technology arrives, maintenance and ongoing support are often left out of the process control plan, and quality of delivery and service suffers. When the local supermarket petrol station introduced a 'fast card' payment system at the pump, the time taken to fill up with petrol (a major CTQ, next to cost, convenience and loyalty reward) was cut dramatically. Within a year, however, the failure rate of the system in accepting cards or issuing printed receipts rose to almost 50 per cent (based on the author's experience), and the new process often took longer than the old one did. New technology often brings facilities that 'delight' and exceed expectations. Such facilities rapidly become expected, and part of the criteria set that defines acceptable quality standards. Some of the cost savings gained from increased volume of business (vehicles on the forecourt for less time) and reduced staff costs (fewer customer interactions and fewer cash-based transactions) must be ploughed back into technical support to keep the new process performing. Total failure of the system for two months (and for no apparent reason) left a string of disgruntled customers with no option but to return to queuing at the payment desk and muttering their dissatisfaction to each other. As is often the case, the staff were not at fault, but still had to endure both extra work and customer complaints. What was once an unexpected delight was now a necessity, and failure of such features can force otherwise loyal customers to go elsewhere. Had this new process change been designed and commissioned within a working Six Sigma quality initiative, it is less likely that failure would have been allowed to occur and to affect customer satisfaction to such an extent. It would also have ensured that employees were empowered to deal with the issue in the short term, and perhaps instigate a quality improvement project to remove the causes for failure in the long term. Only by correctly applying the best in new technological advances, clearly directed towards improving process efficiency and quality, can any organization aspire to be indeed world-class.

CONCLUSION

In the search for a Six Sigma level of customer quality, the goal of any organization must be to become both more competitive and more efficient than rival businesses, and the essence of competitiveness is to be consistently faster, better, easier to do business with, and cheaper. To be better than anyone else in every respect can be a challenge, but certainly implies that customers would be foolish to go anywhere else.

Six Sigma was born from a need to compete in an environment that now demands ever-increasing levels of efficiency and product or service perfection. No longer is it possible to be successful in the long term without placing quality in a central position in corporate strategy, and it is this necessity that is perhaps the main reason for the undoubted success of the Six Sigma approach.

For quality to take centre-stage in any organization requires more than just a new quality department, or a new slogan, or an excursion into quality circles or Total Quality Management. Standing on its own, each contributing aspect that forms Six Sigma as a composite whole will certainly fail to deliver long-term results. Only by combining the actively customer-centric approach, Total Quality Management tools, proactive cultural and management change, the target of Six Sigma performance and a statistical measurement approach to improving processes can an organization find all the elements for an assured strategy paving the way to excellent customer quality.

Easy gains can be made early on in any Six Sigma initiative, and excellent improvements can be seen as a result of simple changes. To continue to extend the differentiating gap that excellent quality brings implies a need to continually re-invent both processes and levels of quality.

Six Sigma is a journey towards a new level of true customer quality that has only just begun, but the early signs of the great potential to come are already visible.

SUMMARY

- A mastery of Six Sigma principles is necessary in order to go beyond the natural limit of process improvement via 'ordinary' quality projects.
- Processes that are core to customer satisfaction and quality should be aligned to customers, and managed and controlled by a process-owner. The use of Statistical Process Control together with appropriate action plans will ensure day-to-day delivery to CTQ characteristics, and long-term management and improvement will ensure continued success and viability.
- Organizations naturally seem to level out at a process performance of between two and three sigma, and a higher level is both attainable and maintainable. Process improvement of up to about four sigma is relatively easy to achieve using simple quality improvement projects based on standard TQM practices.
- Four sigma performance is often a limit set by inherent capabilities of the process, and progressing beyond four sigma demands greater skill and ingenuity. Simple effort alone will often fail to provide satisfactory results against the diminishing returns, and the use of process redesign and (new) technology becomes necessary.

- Redesigning processes is a powerful way to extend Six Sigma quality beyond a four sigma performance. It can enable proactive gains in customer service or new products, and yet remain a cost-effective way to use quality teams. It also extends inherent process capability, and can improve the management of the interaction between multiple CTQ characteristics.
- Appropriate use of technology to improve efficiency and meet customer CTQs is essential in reaching Six Sigma quality in the long term. New technology enables greater efficiency, lower error rates and the ability to redesign processes to meet customer needs more effectively. The use and application of technology must be business-driven and well supported to achieve real benefits from improved efficiency and customer quality.

Appendix

During the 1990s, a number of large multinational organizations took on the challenge of Six Sigma quality, and it is to be expected that many more businesses will wish to do so during the first decade of the new century. Over the relatively short interval of time since Six Sigma was first conceived at Motorola, application has been principally within large manufacturing companies, and the question therefore remains how best to apply Six Sigma elsewhere.

This Appendix gives some guidance about introducing and using Six Sigma in a range of organizations, from small and medium-sized businesses to large multinationals. Each organization will have its own strengths and difficulties, some of which may only become apparent during the introduction and application of Six Sigma quality. There are real benefits to be gained from any Total Quality Management initiative, and one of the major advantages of Six Sigma is the ability to introduce a common metric of customer-perceived quality, which should be applicable to any size and type of organization. Six Sigma is also about the spirit of excellent customer service, and can be applied anywhere, even without the use of statistics or control charts, although this is likely to detract from the full impact and benefit of having a scientific, reproducible and common metric.

The important points for any successful implementation of Six Sigma quality, regardless of company size, are:

- strong, visible leadership;
- involvement for all;
- a strong customer focus;
- a statistical basis for measurement;
- substantial process improvement;
- sufficient resources;
- ongoing process control.

IMPLEMENTING SIX SIGMA IN SMALL ORGANIZATIONS

The challenge of Six Sigma for a small organization of less than 30 staff concerns resources and structure. TQM has always typically involved project teams or quality circles, and many small businesses will simply not have the necessary staff to form even one team. It is always assumed that benefits accrue from having a team of employees, but practical experience with such teams shows that there are many drawbacks, and small organizations should never shy away from formal quality management simply because of considerations of size. The benefits small size brings are speed, leanness and flexibility in responding to change. In general, smaller organizations will also have a reduced management structure, with perhaps one important figurehead at the top. Where businesses are 'family-run', change directed from the top can be implemented with great speed, and obstacles and difficulties more easily overcome. Conversely, of course, such influential people have to be totally and visibly in favour of Six Sigma, and must consciously delegate control of process improvement to other staff. In many respects, the biggest upheaval required for Six Sigma may lie with the boss at the top.

The temptation for the smaller organization will be to jump into process quality improvements far too quickly. It is far more important for the smaller organization to ensure that every iota of effort is directed exactly where it is needed for maximum benefit, so an overall quality strategy plan is vital right from the start. It can generally be assumed that smaller companies are closer to the customer base, and may already be exhibiting excellent quality management and control. Six Sigma is about overall management, strategy, culture and change, and the organization needs first to build all of this into a sound corporate strategy plan. If no such plan exists, then a thorough appraisal of the business, operation, market and customer base should be undertaken as a first step. This can be coupled with introducing the more technical aspects of Six Sigma quality to just the senior management and key staff at this stage. The formation of a company strategy plan will in itself bring many advantages, but ultimately, such a plan will serve to ensure that quality is applied for the benefit of all, and in a well-ordered way.

It is as well to bring in some form of external consultancy support for the first few steps in introducing Six Sigma, which may last two or more years. Not only will technical support be required, as it is unlikely that the organization will have statisticians in-house, but an external point of view will be essential, to acquire a balanced assessment of strengths and weaknesses. External help and assistance will be required for much of the practical operation of Six Sigma methodology, in such areas as customer research, data collection and analysis, and quality project implementation. For this to be effective, guidance and assistance needs to be well planned and integrated on a 'just in time' basis.

The learning curve for Six Sigma is steep, and with fewer staff to absorb facts and details, it will not be possible to compress the implementation without inducing overload. Smaller organizations may choose to restrict the degree to which their own employees become immersed in the technical practicalities. Involvement in itself is a good thing (if not essential), but may take too much time and remove essential personnel from their day-to-day tasks. A sensible balance is required, as continually taking all the exciting aspects away from in-house staff will lead to a distinct loss of fun and interest. Much of the positive momentum and enthusiasm from Six Sigma is gained from actually conducting process improvements. It may well be a good idea to take on part-time or temporary staff to free up internal employees for the quality effort, and this can be carried out in a very positive way to imply worth and investment for the long term, and thus improve staff loyalty. By such means, the entire company structure can be rapidly opened up, and it will send a clear signal to all that the company is taking Six Sigma seriously. Long-standing employees can also be highly motivated, and most able to contribute and execute quality and process improvements.

Clearly, such an investment in external consultancy, additional services and staffing resources must be balanced by meaningful and positive bottom-line benefits, and very early on in the initiative. The strategy plan for the company must show non-quality-related routes by which the business intends to grow and expand or acquire more revenue. By linking such non-quality benefits to the quality initiative, it becomes possible both to enhance the impact of planned strategies, and to effect a better implementation and cost justification.

Six Sigma involves cultural change and upheaval, as does any Total Quality Management initiative. By running quality and other less palatable or exciting changes in parallel, the positive benefits and revenue gained can often outweigh less desirable changes and costs. If the company wishes to grow in staff numbers, for example, encouraging temporary staff and job movement to accommodate short-term quality initiatives is an excellent way to open up new positions, move experienced staff around, and look for new employees. On the other hand, bringing in new blood and external consultants can be very unsettling for some long-standing employees, and a proportion may wish to move on rather than be saddled with what they deem 'inappropriate' customer quality and change. Loss of staff can be both a benefit and a burden, and such side issues must be investigated and fully considered before launching Six Sigma. The only certainty is that it will be a period of change, and the senior manager must know what particular strategy and agenda will be adhered to throughout. Six Sigma is never the final goal in itself, but must become part of a well-developed strategy of general business improvement.

The choice of external consultants needs to be taken with some care, as a small organization may not wish to use large (and expensive) general consultancy firms. Specific needs must be identified and targeted, such as statistical analysis, specific training and motivation, strategy development, and perhaps above all, practical implementation. When a small organization reaches out for assistance, it must ensure that advice can be backed up with competent facilitation and support for implementation. The smaller, independent consultancy can often offer both sound advice and real practical support, and may be more able to provide a one-to-one service over many years, particularly with direct coaching and support. No small company will be able by itself to retain a Six Sigma expert, particularly as the services of such a person are likely to be required little but often over several years. As Six Sigma quality becomes more widely adopted in the UK and Europe, the services of such experts will become increasingly available, and hence counter the tendency for Six Sigma to become the reserve of the big and wealthy.

Success with Six Sigma in the smaller organization will come with an adherence to the spirit of Six Sigma, even if not the practice. It is as well to leave the statistics to others, and to get firmly involved with process improvement and developing excellent customer service. After all, financial returns come from efficient processes and excellent quality, not an in-house understanding of statistics and normal curves. Such expertise can always be bought in from somewhere, and the small company must capitalize on its own skills and knowledge. The best financial returns will come from just one or two critical factors that have the major and most direct impact on customer quality. Every customer is different, and the entire marketplace may hold many types and classes of customer, each with their own peculiar requirements. By nature, small organizations target a more manageable subset of the entire customer population, and so need worry less about customer diversity. The small organization will also have the advantage of excellence in all that it does, which can attract a high price premium. Success will come by keeping close to the customer and locating the vital few CTQs which matter most or can most easily be improved. Targeting and delivering on these alone will give outstanding returns, and may even allow price differentials to be increased compared to larger organizations.

Running quality projects in a small business will certainly be a challenge, and it may be more appropriate to work with just one or two staff, together with an external agent of change. The purpose of quality project teams is to ensure appropriate and correct application of Six Sigma ideals and practices, as well as effective process improvement. Using cross-functional teams in larger organizations ensures that good ideas are sought, developed and correctly brought to bear on the issues. In smaller organizations, a lack of ideas can be overcome by broad-range benchmarking against competitors and similar industries, and by using external consultants and trade advice. Indeed, a view from one external person may provide more insight and fresh ideas than a large internal team ever could. Only very large organizations can afford research and development, but it does not require industrial espionage to find out what is happening in the market. Customers themselves are often very well informed, particularly in the niche markets, where they may actively seek out the smaller company for 'quality' and 'better service'. The smaller organization can capitalize on this benefit and listen hard to customers. It may even be possible to invite one or two selected customers to participate actively in the quality initiative. A substantial proportion of the total customer market is generally in favour of local and smaller business, and often only fails to place trade with such organizations because of cost or convenience factors on offer elsewhere. Such loyalty can be both used in Six Sigma and capitalized upon.

A change from tiered management to process-ownership is likely to be foreign to the small entrepreneurial organization, and will become a major issue from the very beginning if process improvements cannot be developed and implemented freely. It is important that process improvement is effective in its conception as well as its execution, and undue influence and pressure from the one at the top can easily ruin any project. The aim must be to keep the management of strategy and business control separate from the operational management. This allows the top manager to steer the organization without affecting the ability of (other) process-owners to adapt and modify their own processes. Even very large organizations know how dominant family relationships in the boardroom can restrict the ability of operational managers to effect much-needed process change.

The longer-term benefit from Six Sigma will be seen in the move away from 'gut feeling' and management by influence towards management by facts and figures. What is ultimately required is a definite split between management of the corporate strategy by plan, and the management of operations by adherence to measurements of quality characteristics critical to the customer. Only in the very smallest businesses, where many roles are compressed into a sole trader or two-person partnership, will such change be difficult to implement.

It must always be kept in mind that small can be beautiful, and many larger organizations are learning the need to divide themselves into more manageable, flexible and responsive business units. Growth often brings inefficiency, and many small companies are brought to ruin as victims of their own success. Even if only the spirit of Six Sigma is adhered to, it will ensure that the customer comes first, and that businesses will always keep customer quality and satisfaction to the forefront.

THE CHALLENGE OF SIX SIGMA IN MEDIUM-SIZED ENTERPRISES

It can be difficult to decide exactly what constitutes a medium-sized enterprise, but perhaps a good guide is one with 50 to 500 or so employees. At such a level of staffing, it becomes possible to dedicate (at least) one person to quality full-time, and thus reduce, if not eliminate, the reliance upon external change agents. It will also be much easier to gather five or so employees to form quality teams without totally decimating any one critical department, and to establish a broader cross-section from the organization in doing so. Typically, such organizations as General Electric have identified the need for 2–4 per cent of all staff to be associated full-time with quality, and indeed 50 staff seems to be about the break-even point where this just becomes possible. The larger organization of 200 or 300 can therefore afford to retain a quality manager/director as well as several other Six Sigma experts and practitioners, and much more emphasis can then be placed on ensuring that the practice of TQM and Six Sigma is applied universally and correctly.

One difficulty that arises with size will be greater resistance to the new quality initiative and change. As organizations grow in numbers, it becomes easier for individuals to cultivate disinterest and non-participation, both active and passive. Clearly, in small organizations, if one visible and important person is actively against Six Sigma, then this attitude must change or the quality initiative will be a non-starter. If such people exist lower down, buried in the hierarchy of a larger company, resistance and disinterest can go undetected or unchallenged until much later, when it can easily trap the unwary and halt quality projects mid-stream. Here, the influence and involvement of all staff is an issue, and the launch and presentation of Six Sigma becomes of paramount importance. Again, the people at the very top of the organization need to be visibly supportive of every aspect of quality and change, and must demonstrate by their actions that such support is more than lip service. By using quality project teams, the initiative will also spread from the bottom up throughout the organization, and the critical area now becomes middle management. In larger companies, operational management and responsibility can be combined with company strategy and policy deployment in the same people. If such middle management is not wholly in favour of Six Sigma and all that it stands for, problems will undoubtedly arise at some point. It is perhaps useful to introduce the ideas and concepts involved to all senior staff who hold controlling and influencing positions at an early stage, and to conduct a strategy of persuasion and structural alteration in preparation for the new process management structure to come.

The medium-sized organization is more likely to have a strategy plan, and perhaps even successful quality initiatives and practices, already in place. Early work should be applied to considering how best to integrate both Six Sigma and existing quality strategies, and what the principal goals will be for the quality programme over both the short and long term. External consultancy is still likely to be highly desirable, at least for the preparation and launch stages, and should be used to both educate and influence. With dedicated, full-time internal staff, there must be more emphasis on knowledge and skill transfer from the external agents to the company, and part of the strategy plan must be to ensure that the organization becomes self-supporting as soon as is practically appropriate. Larger size will mean that more projects can be undertaken concurrently, and there may be value in trading off such early self-sufficiency against retaining external support for longer, and thus driving the quality initiative broader and faster during the first stages. Considerable value is gained from the rapid spread of knowledge and experience of Six Sigma throughout the organization, and thereby quickly eliminating pockets of fear and uncertainty where cynicism can grow and take hold. If only a few are involved at the start, and quality execution becomes either cliquey or shrouded in mystery, resistance will certainly build. Since Six Sigma theory is statistical by nature and the terminology and techniques are rather bizarre to the uninitiated, doubt and scepticism will always result, no matter how much effort is devoted to spreading awareness. The only sensible answer is to get everyone involved as soon as possible, and to drive the inevitable 'doubting Thomases' into a small minority where they can ultimately do little real harm.

The choice of who will become the expert internal staff is very important, and ideally, such people should come from within the organization and already show both promise and enthusiasm. Helpful characteristics to look for are strong leadership skills, a positive influence within the organization, an understanding of statistical theory (or an ability to learn about it), team skills, good problem-solving aptitudes, and the ability to work at all levels of the organization and with suppliers, customers and external consultants. This is indeed a tall order, particularly as a good understanding of the business and its operational functions will also be required, so it may be that much early work will have to be expended on identifying, developing and supporting such employees. In the end, this effort will benefit the organization and the quality initiative many times over.

The opportunity for payback provided by Six Sigma increases in proportion to the size and complexity of the organization. In the short term, small and already efficient businesses (particularly non-manufacturing) may have difficulty in making Six Sigma quality pay for itself by means of process improvements alone. This will not be the case when employee numbers run into the hundreds, as processes will naturally have evolved in myriad ways, each of which moves further away from the customer and more and more towards keeping other functions at a safe distance. Plenty of quick-hit solutions will be waiting for discovery, each of which can easily return cost savings in the very short term to balance the expense of staff involvement and process changes. Such freely available bounty needs to be used to expand the quality initiative to all corners of the organization, and to ensure that process improvement is not just about cost savings, but also about customer-related improvement. The larger organization may also have moved away from direct contact with the customer, and may have sub-contracted many routine tasks to other companies. It can be tempting to ignore the vital work required in obtaining 'voice of the customer' material, and then acting upon it, and the medium-sized organization suffers the disadvantage of lacking large corporate resources to allocate effort to such items as human resources and employee surveys. Six Sigma and TQM are about people, which includes employees as well as customers. Small organizations can often easily talk to both, perhaps even by standing in one physical location for a few days. It is said that if one stands in the same place long enough, all the world will pass by. Very small and very large organizations may well be able to apply this principle, but the company of medium size will have to work hardest to hear everyone within an appropriate time scale. If the organization does not already survey customers and employees, or provide regular staff training and assessment, then this is a very good time to start, and it is as well to commence some of this work before the Six Sigma quality initiative begins in earnest.

Larger organizations can reap benefits from Six Sigma which extend beyond the boundaries of internal processes by involving major customers and suppliers. With a larger customer and supplier base, a small proportion of them may be responsible for the considerable majority of trade, both within and outside the company. Strong working relationships between the business and critical customers and suppliers can be improved through the use of quality scorecards, and even involvement within the quality initiative itself. Setting up a very positive TQM programme with a visible 'Six Sigma' banner makes the task of instigating such initiatives much easier. Since quality is all about improving the satisfaction and esteem of customers and suppliers, 'showing off' in a positive way can also heighten the internal benefits.

It may well be a good idea for organizations to avoid using the esoteric terminology of Six Sigma, and to treat it as far as possible as a more straightforward quality initiative. How this is achieved depends upon past experiences with quality and customer service, current involvement with such initiatives as ISO 9000, and local cultural variations and circumstances. Quality circles, Black Belts and passing management whims and fancies have long since moved into the domain of the cartoon comic strip. The 'Dilbert' cartoon character is quite familiar with Six Sigma and TQM, and can be found lampooning the 'dead fish' diagram, quality circles and Black Belts from time to time. Ishikawa did not devise the cause-and-effect diagram with the sole purpose of amusing (although it does indeed look like a dead fish), but as a working tool to help with quality teamwork. This does not prevent a proportion of those in any organization resorting to mirth at the expense of quality and those involved. The British fondness for the Christmas pantomime is perhaps not understood or shared by the rest of the world, and is indeed logically totally bizarre. How can anyone explain why a woman plays the principal man, and a man plays the principal dame? Green spotlight, boo, hiss and cries of 'It's behind you!' ... Confused? The point is that when children who know nothing else take it at face value, and when adults who know it is inane accept that but still join in, suddenly it becomes a lot of fun – *and it works*. The same applies to Six Sigma. There is a very real need to create a critical mass of acceptance, and for cries of 'Come on in – the water is lovely!', even if it does not look that inviting. Perhaps only an Englishman could possibly suggest that Disneyworld is not all that wonderful because it is 'not real, and too artificial', and many do regard Six Sigma as just another passing 'American management whim'. The arguments for adopting Six Sigma in full, or for altering phrases, names and titles, only really matter if long-term external compliance is required. If the organization expects to recruit new employees with Six Sigma experience, or to be able to be seen by outsiders as using Six Sigma in practice, full compliance should be undertaken. Whatever it takes, organizations must ensure that a critical mass of support is rapidly generated and spread throughout the company, and that Six Sigma is taken seriously and applied correctly.

For the more complex and functionally based business, the subtle move towards a new process structure aligned to the customer must be an essential long-term vision of the quality initiative. Process-ownership, at least as an enlightened concept, is perhaps more important in the long term than any other aspect of Six Sigma quality. The rush of enthusiasm and tangible benefits from any TQM initiative always seem to bud, bloom, wither and eventually perish. Even the driest deserts burst into a riot of colour when the annual rains come, but once they have passed, the only things that survive are the seeds for the future. To ensure a continual crop of benefits, the inherent company structure must change to allow maximum efficiency, total customer alignment, excellent performance to customer-related measurements, effective and appropriate control, and above all, the speed of flexibility for future change. If an organization has slowly grown over time into a state of inefficiency and poor customer quality, only a radical new approach to management will ensure that history is not repeated once the Six Sigma initiative has become outmoded, as it inevitably will.

With the increased size and depth of resources, the medium-sized organization needs to ensure that Six Sigma quality is applied fully and correctly, and in so doing will gain from the full spectrum of benefits that such an undertaking brings. Six Sigma should be used as the firm base upon which the company can grow, both in size and strength.

EXPERIENCES IN LARGE, GLOBAL ORGANIZATIONS

Six Sigma emerged from one particular multinational during the 1990s, and has since predominantly remained with such large, diverse (and American) organizations. There can be no doubt that as companies grow in size, the benefits to be gained as well as the pitfalls from implementing Six Sigma also increase in magnitude. When large companies cross real or imaginary boundaries and divisions, of necessity it then becomes the turn of the quality initiative itself to adapt and change. Rigidity in an organization leads to inefficiency and poor quality – why should this be any different for Six Sigma itself?

Six Sigma is not generally introduced for its own sake, but for ulterior motives, such as structural change and increased revenue and profits. What come from Six Sigma are results and successes, where results may be tangible cost savings and defect-reductions, and successes perhaps associated with an agenda of organizational change and renewal. Six Sigma, if applied with some gusto and sincerity, will always return some form of practical result, and some of the adopting companies have experienced quite astounding breakthroughs where other TQM initiatives have failed in the past. Success in less tangible areas is, however, another matter.

As noted in an article from *USA Today* (D. Jones, 'Firms aim for Six Sigma efficiency', 21 July 1998), the success of Six Sigma has not always been plain sailing. IBM undertook a Six Sigma quality initiative during the early 1990s, although it is now almost impossible to tell, as the attempt was quickly abandoned when John Akers, the then championing CEO, left in 1993. Lockheed Martin tried Six Sigma at about the same time, but the initiative floundered first time around, and a re-launch necessitated calling the experts 'Program Managers' rather than 'Black Belts', to avoid jokes and scepticism. Adopted by over thirty companies by 1998, its impact has varied from one organization to another, but more recently it has been the involvement of AlliedSignal and General Electric that has captured most of the attention.

To launch Six Sigma in General Electric, Jack Welsh imposed not only (up to) a 40 per cent stake of senior management salary and bonus that would be related to quality performance, but also insisted (after the initiative had gained hold) that nobody would be promoted at executive level without Six Sigma training and experience. Extensive resources were made available in terms of training and employee involvement, and from the very start each quality project had anticipated cost savings tied into future profit figures. It rapidly became very difficult to either avoid Six Sigma or to invent savings that could not be quickly substantiated on the bottom line. General Electric also has the benefit of substantial corporate groups for, among other things, quality and internal audit, and such resources can quickly locate, devise and spread best practices, support and new ideas.

The real problems facing very large organizations which wish to adopt Six Sigma revolve around the need to ensure total and rapid involvement, as insufficient drive will result in patchy take-up, while on the other hand, overly strong leadership and initial zeal can become restrictive and divisive. If one success from introducing Six Sigma is a common metric and approach to customer quality, then this is only substantiated by handing out the songsheet and making sure that everyone sings the same tune. Such was the very early mania and incentive for Six Sigma in General Electric that there was a tendency to label everything a quality project. Every design or IT project with a budget of over $1 million had to be a Design For Six Sigma (DFSS) project, which automatically extended the initial work by months, if not years, and added a burden of up-front training and resource requirements that could not always be met. The danger is that the spirit of excellent customer quality drowns in the rigour of the imposed and fully audited corporate methodology. Although it rapidly became required and enforced policy to conduct DFSS projects, without training, support and mentoring, such undertakings flounder, and early DFSS training was almost impossible to obtain in Europe for many critical months.

Nowhere is the need for cultural adaptation more evident than in the global launch of a single initiative such as Six Sigma. Taken initially from American resources and material, the natural diversity encountered in European countries required adaptation beyond just simple language translation. The difference between manufacturing and pure service industry is also deep-seated, and in taking Six Sigma from core manufacturing, GE Capital made a number of subtle changes, and in the process gained valuable insight into change strategy.

In terms of the list of necessities at the beginning of this Appendix, General Electric is a very laudable example, and has scored highly indeed on the following points:

- outstanding leadership, both at the very top and (even if coerced) in every division and business unit;
- all-encompassing employee involvement, in a structured and well-managed way, using a tiered approach of experts, practitioners and general quality teams;

- exceptional customer focus, with all projects targeting either external or internal customer needs, and hence directly influencing both the perception and reality of quality, the aim being to ensure that the customer 'feels the quality';
- strong adherence to a full statistical approach, even in non-manufacturing divisions;
- real and positive process improvements, driven by defect-reduction and cost-efficiency, with firm monitoring of project results;
- application of sufficient resources to launch and maintain the momentum, and a long-term investment in new quality departments to ensure ongoing support;
- radical alteration to business structure to ensure ongoing process control managed by (new) process-owners.

The success in the short term has been impressive. The question is: what will happen to such organizations and Six Sigma over the longer term? What is Six Sigma really about, and can this variant of quality management continue to evolve and adapt and yet still deliver? It is tempting to suggest that as Six Sigma is about cultural and management change, then unless real and deep-seated transformation has taken place in such companies, in the long term the enthusiasm and drive for customer quality will wane, just as it has for TQM in general. To the list of necessities must therefore be added one further point: a genuine and active willingness to adapt and modify attitudes and management practices. Successful organizations which wish to make Six Sigma a real and ongoing journey of continual quality improvement will need to become more spontaneous and adaptive, just as small entrepreneurial businesses are today. This must include the way in which TQM and Six Sigma evolve and are applied and used within the organization itself.

DPMO-TO-PROCESS SIGMA CONVERSION TABLE

The process sigma metric is formally calculated from the number of standard deviations (sigma) which fit between the mean and the acceptable customer limit for a process, providing the process performance follows a pattern similar to that of the normal distribution. The part (or tail) of the normal distribution which falls outside of the customer limit equates to the defects experienced by the customer, the whole distribution equating to all possible opportunities for such a defect. This can also be described as a fractional part of a million, often referred to as the Defects Per Million Opportunities, or DPMO. This fraction of the normal distribution falling outside of a given process sigma can be found from pre-calculated tables, and can be applied to situations where the process shows a non-normal distribution or is more complex. Once a 'defect' and an 'opportunity for a defect' have been defined and counted, it is often much easier to both use and understand the DPMO-to-process sigma conversion table than it is to formally calculate the process sigma from the actual distribution. Without having to understand normal curves, means and standard deviations, Table A.1 allows anyone with a simple calculator and a count of 'defects' and 'opportunities for defect' to arrive at a process sigma value, for any process.

Note that Table A.1 includes the standard 1.5 sigma shift for short-term sigma. To convert between short-term sigma (the best possible process capability) and long-term sigma (or process performance, which is equivalent to the number of standard deviations between customer limit and mean), subtract 1.5 from the sigma-value given in the table. Values in the table have been rounded to four or less significant figures, and will have some degree of inaccuracy, although it is unlikely that greater significance will ever be either appropriate or needed.

Table A.1 DPMO-to-process sigma conversion table

Process sigma	0.00	0.01	0.02	0.03	0.04	0.05	0.06	0.07	0.08	0.09
	Defects Per Million Opportunities									
0.0	933200	931900	930600	929200	927900	926500	925100	923600	922200	920700
0.1	919200	917700	916200	914700	913100	911500	909900	908200	906600	904900
0.2	903200	901500	899700	898000	896200	894400	892500	890700	888800	886900
0.3	884900	883000	881000	879000	877000	874900	872900	870800	868600	866500
0.4	864300	862100	859900	857700	855400	853100	850800	848500	846100	843800
0.5	841300	838900	836500	834000	831500	828900	826400	823800	821200	818600
0.6	815900	813300	810600	807800	805100	802300	799500	796700	793900	791000
0.7	788100	785200	782300	779400	776400	773400	770400	767300	764200	761100
0.8	758000	754900	751700	748600	745400	742200	738900	735700	732400	729100
0.9	725700	722400	719000	715700	712300	708800	705400	701900	698500	695000
1.0	691500	687900	684400	680800	677200	673600	670000	666400	662800	659100
1.1	655400	651700	648000	644300	640600	636800	633100	629300	625500	621700
1.2	617900	614100	610300	606400	602600	598700	594800	591000	587100	583200
1.3	579300	575300	571400	567500	563600	559600	555700	551700	547800	543800
1.4	539800	535900	531900	527900	523900	519900	516000	512000	508000	504000
1.5	500000	496000	492000	488000	484000	480100	476100	472100	468100	464100
1.6	460200	456200	452200	448300	444300	440400	436400	432500	428600	424700
1.7	420700	416800	412900	409000	405200	401300	397400	393600	389700	385900
1.8	382100	378300	374500	370700	366900	363200	359400	355700	352000	348300
1.9	344600	340900	337200	333600	330000	326400	322800	319200	315600	312100
2.0	308500	305000	301500	298100	294600	291200	287700	284300	281000	277600
2.1	274300	270900	267600	264300	261100	257800	254600	251400	248300	245100
2.2	242000	238900	235800	232700	229600	226600	223600	220600	217700	214800
2.3	211900	209000	206100	203300	200500	197700	194900	192200	189400	186700
2.4	184100	181400	178800	176200	173600	171100	168500	166000	163500	161100
2.5	158700	156200	153900	151500	149200	146900	144600	142300	140100	137900
2.6	135700	133500	131400	129200	127100	125100	123000	121000	119000	117000
2.7	115100	113100	111200	109300	107500	105600	103800	102000	100300	98530
2.8	96800	95100	93420	91760	90120	88510	86920	85340	83790	82260
2.9	80760	79270	77800	76360	74930	73530	72150	70780	69440	68110
3.0	66810	65520	64260	63010	61780	60570	59380	58210	57050	55920
3.1	54800	53700	52620	51550	50500	49470	48460	47460	46480	45510
3.2	44570	43630	42720	41820	40930	40060	39200	38360	37540	36730
3.3	35930	35150	34380	33620	32880	32160	31440	30740	30050	29380
3.4	28720	28070	27430	26800	26190	25590	25000	24420	23850	23300
3.5	22750	22220	21690	21180	20680	20180	19700	19230	18760	18310
3.6	17860	17430	17000	16590	16180	15780	15390	15000	14630	14260
3.7	13900	13550	13210	12870	12550	12220	11910	11600	11300	11010
3.8	10720	10440	10170	9903	9642	9387	9137	8894	8656	8424
3.9	8198	7976	7760	7549	7344	7143	6947	6756	6569	6387
4.0	6210	6037	5868	5703	5543	5386	5234	5085	4940	4799
4.1	4661	4527	4397	4269	4145	4025	3907	3793	3681	3573
4.2	3467	3364	3264	3167	3072	2980	2890	2803	2718	2635
4.3	2555	2477	2401	2327	2256	2186	2118	2052	1988	1926
4.4	1866	1807	1750	1695	1641	1589	1538	1489	1441	1395
4.5	1350	1306	1264	1223	1183	1144	1107	1070	1035	1001
4.6	968	936	904	874	845	816	789	762	736	711
4.7	687	664	641	619	598	577	557	538	519	501
4.8	483	467	450	434	419	404	390	376	362	350
4.9	337	325	313	302	291	280	270	260	251	242
5.0	233	224	216	208	200	193	185	179	172	165
5.1	159	153	147	142	136	131	126	121	117	112
5.2	108	104	100	96	92	88	85	82	78	75
5.3	72	70	67	64	62	59	57	54	52	50
5.4	48	46	44	42	41	39	37	36	34	33
5.5	32	30	29	28	27	26	25	24	23	22
5.6	21	20	19	18	17	17	16	15	15	14
5.7	13	13	12	12	11	11	10	10	9	9
5.8	9	8	8	7	7	7	7	6	6	6
5.9	5	5	5	5	5	4	4	4	4	4
6.0	3.4	3.2	3.1	3.0	2.8	2.7	2.6	2.4	2	2

To calculate any given value, the following formulae can be used in *Excel* or a similar spread-sheet. NORMSDIST is the standard normal cumulative distribution (the area under the standard normal curve for a given value of z), and NORMSINV is the inverse of the standard normal cumulative distribution. For *Excel* (as for most software), the multiplication symbol is * and the division symbol is /. Rounding can usually be applied by specifying a number format for the cell.

The equation for converting DPMO to process sigma is:

$$process\ sigma = \text{NORMSINV}(1 - (dpmo/1\,000\,000)) + 1.5$$

The equation for converting process sigma to DPMO is:

$$dpmo = 1\,000\,000 * (1 - \text{NORMSDIST}(process\ sigma - 1.5))$$

Index

The Gower Handbook of Management

Fourth Edition

Edited by Dennis Lock

'If you have only one management book on your shelf, this must be the one.'

Dennis Lock recalls launching the first edition in 1983 with this aim in mind. It has remained the guiding principle behind subsequent editions, and today *The Gower Handbook of Management* is widely regarded as a manager's bible: an authoritative, gimmick-free and practical guide to best practice in management. By covering the broadest possible range of subjects, this *Handbook* replicates in book form a forum in which managers can meet experts from a range of professional disciplines.

The new edition features:

- 65 expert contributors - many of them practising managers and all of them recognized authorities in their field;
- many new contributors: over one-third are new to this edition;
- 72 chapters, of which half are completely new;
- 20 chapters on subjects new to this edition; and
- a brand new design and larger format.

The Gower Handbook of Management has received many plaudits during its distinguished career, summed up in the following review from *Director*:

'... packed with information which can be used either as a reference work on a specific problem or as a guide to an entire operation. In a short review one can touch only lightly on the richness and excellence of this book, which well deserves a place on any executive bookshelf.'

Gower

The Organizational Measurement Manual

David Wealleans

The Organizational Measurement Manual is a step-by-step guide to creating performance measurements at the working level. It addresses the procedures for identifying, designing, monitoring and using measurements and how these might relate to other objectives and initiatives within an organization. In so doing it explores the use of general performance measurement as a management tool for the key areas of control, customer satisfaction and business improvement.

The book is clearly differentiated from many other publications on the subject of measurement by the firm distinction made between general, strategic measurement that represents an umbrella approach to the quantification of performance and the monitoring of process-level attributes that directly relate to the performance of an individual work team. The benefits of, and best practice approach to, the use of process-level measurements are clearly explained.

Gower

A Practical Guide to Business Process Re-Engineering

Mike Robson and Philip Ullah

Most managers will by now have some understanding of Business Process Re-Engineering and the immense benefits it is capable of bringing. Here at last is a detailed guide to realizing those benefits.

The authors begin with a warning to think carefully about whether the BPR approach is suitable for your particular organization. They go on to show how it can be planned and implemented in a systematic way. With the aid of examples and illustrations they take the reader through the various stages involved, introducing both the principles and the techniques that apply. Finally they explain how to ensure sustained improvement by managing the changes achieved.

Anyone responsible for improving business effectiveness will find the book a worthwhile investment.

Gower

A Project-by-Project Approach to Quality

A Practical Handbook for Individuals, Teams and Organizations

Richard Capper

Do any of the following sound familiar?

You are being given more and more projects, have had little training and seem to start new projects from scratch, taking a different approach each time.
You've just been given a project team to lead and are wondering where to start.
Your team has got multiple priorities and little time or resources - you need to identify the vital few projects and get these moving.
Your organization has flirted with quality, you think the ideas are sound but you can't seem to make the link between the idea and actual change.

Richard Capper's highly practical book will help you to deal with these and many other problems relating to quality. In step-by-step fashion he explains how to set up and manage successful quality projects, how to get other people involved and committed, and how to make project meetings productive. He provides detailed guidance on collecting and using data, piloting your ideas and consolidating the gains you make. The text is supported by action checklists, ready-made formats and real-life case histories. There is also a section of tools and techniques which shows not only how to use different methods but when each one is appropriate.

This comprehensive guide to best practice will benefit anyone determined to achieve lasting improvement individually, in their team or organization.

Gower

Successful TQM

Inside Stories from European Quality Award Winners

Edited by Klaus J Zink

The ideas behind Total Quality Management have been known and applied for many years. In many companies the approach has failed, but in others it has been a spectacular success.

This book reveals how some of Europe's best known companies - most of them winners of the prestigious European Quality Award - set about planning and implementing their own TQM programmes. In each case the story is told by someone intimately involved with the implementation and together they provide a unique insight into the entire process. The companies include Hewlett Packard, KLM, IBM, Rank Xerox, Texas Instruments, TNT Express and SGS Thomson.

The book is further supplemented by an opening chapter by Professor Zink, a long-time champion of TQM in which he outlines its underlying concepts and describes the European Model.

This remarkable collection is guaranteed to inform and inspire anyone currently travelling on the TQM road to excellence.

Gower